# INTRODUCTION
# TO EASTERN CHRISTIAN
# SPIRITUALITY

# Introduction
# to Eastern Christian
# Spirituality

## The Syriac Tradition

**Chorbishop Seely Beggiani**

**Scranton: The University of Scranton Press**

**Library of Congress Cataloging-in-Publication Data**

Beggiani, Seely, J., 1935 -
  Introduction to Eastern Christian Spirituality : the Syriac
tradition / Seely Beggiani.
      p. cm.
  Includes bibliographical references and index.
  ISBN 0-940866-12-9 (paper)
  1. Spirituality–Eastern churches–History. 2. Eastern churches–
Doctrines–History. 3. Syriac Christians. 4. Fathers of the church, Syriac.
5. Christian literature, Early–Syriac authors–History. I. Title.
BX106.2.B44 1991
248'.088215–dc20                                              90-70702
                                                                  CIP


**Distribution:**

**The University of Scranton Press**
**Linden Street & Monroe Avenue**
**Scranton, PA    18510**
**Phone: 1–800–941–3081**
**Fax: 1–800–941–8804**


**PRINTED IN THE UNITED STATES OF AMERICA**

# Contents

*Nihil obstat:*
Rev. Msgr. John D. Faris, J.O.C.D.
Censor Librorum

*Imprimatur:*
Archbishop Francis Zayek, S.T.D., J.C.D.
Diocese of St. Maron—U.S.A.

28 January 1989: Feast of Saint Ephrem

# Foreword

The study and practice of the spiritual life is the lifelong pursuit of all who seek union with God. At the present time there is a renewed interest in the great spiritual writers and classics of the past. The purpose of this work is to introduce some of the major writers and ascetics of the Syriac world, that region of the Middle East that was the home of the Syriac language and culture. Although it is an area rich in thought and tradition, the Syriac world has not been studied extensively in English and is little known by the general public. Ecclesiastically, it includes the Church of the East and the churches of the early Antiochene tradition. Geographically, it comprises the region stretching from the northeastern Mediterranean coast to the Persian Gulf. The Syriac world is the heir of Judeo–Christianity, the world of St. Ephrem and Isaac of Nineveh.

This work seeks to be a modest introduction to a very abundant and complex heritage. To attempt a thorough study of the major themes and stages of Syriac spirituality would involve more than one dissertation. To do justice to any of the writers cited in this work would involve book-length treatment. Furthermore, the authors cited were not studied in the original Syriac but through translations, and there was much reliance on secondary sources. There are two sources which we chose to use extensively: the *Dictionnaire de Spiritualité*, whose contributors are recognized as world authorities in their subject, and volume seven of the *Woodbrooke Studies: Early Christian Mystics*, edited by A. Mingana, which is the major resource for some of the authors we are studying.

Although he does not belong to the Syriac tradition, Evagrius of Pontus has been included because he had such a pervasive influence on Syriac thought. On the other hand, the Syriac writer who took Evagrius's teachings to extreme conclusions, Stephen Bar Sudaili, is included in an appendix because his position was too extreme and gained little following. Pseudo–Dionysius the Areopagite is included because he most likely originated in the

Syriac region. However, his writings had a far greater influence on the Byzantine and western worlds than on Syriac thinkers.

Finally, we have limited our attention to the early stages of the Syriac spiritual tradition, choosing to draw a line at the eighth century when the major themes of Syriac spirituality had become fairly fixed.

Therefore, this book offers a digest of the thoughts and aspirations of select ascetical writers of the Middle East, their original insights and their principal contributions to Christian spiritual tradition. As an introduction, its goal is to stimulate further interest in and study of Syriac thought.

I am grateful to Maronite Archbishop Francis Zayek, Bishop John Chedid, many friends among the clergy and laity of the Diocese of St. Maron, and my colleagues at Catholic University of America for their inspiration and support. Ms. Laura Way, who acted as editorial associate for this book, was indispensable in its coming to be.

# Acknowledgments

The author wishes to acknowledge the following authors and publishers for permission to use material under copyright:

To Sebastian Brock for permission to use his articles, "Divine Call and Human Response: The Syriac Tradition II: St. Isaac of Nineveh," *The Way* (1981) pp. 68–74; and "The Prayer of the Heart in Syrian Tradition," *Sobornost* 4:2 (London: Fellowship of St. Alban and St. Sergius, 1975) pp. 79–89.

To Cistercian Publications, WMU Station, Kalamazoo, Michigan 49008 for permission to use *The Syriac Fathers on Prayer and the Spiritual Life*, introduced and translated by Sebastian Brock, copyright 1987.

To W. Heffer & Sons Ltd., 20 Trinity Street, Cambridge, England for permission to use *Woodbrooke Studies*, Vol. 7, edited and translated by A. Mingana in 1933.

# Introduction

Reflecting its origins in first-century converts to Christianity, the Syriac world has always rooted its spirituality on the sacred scriptures and the call to total discipleship by Christ. In the first few centuries it tended to develop its own indigenous forms of asceticism. The great father of the Syriac church, St. Ephrem, adopted a moderate attitude. With his incarnational view of creation, he taught that the spiritual vocation was available not only to the celibate but to the married as well and that the spiritual life should be lived within the ecclesial community. The early institution of the "Sons and Daughters of the Covenant" is a witness to this way of thinking.

With John ("the Solitary") of Apamea we have the fruition of early Syriac spiritual theory. Reflecting the Syriac world view, he based both his theology and spirituality on the theme of hope, especially of the future resurrection, and on the implications of the mystery of baptism. Influenced by the scriptures and the writings of St. Paul, he structured the spiritual life according to the threefold division of the human person, namely, the corporeal, the psychic (that is, the lower activities of the soul) and the spiritual. Asceticism, the practice of prayer and the ultimate union with God were understood as the perfecting of this tripartite aspect of the human person.

Classic spiritual thought eventually developed in divergent directions. The Neoplatonic worldview as expressed in Origen and systematized into spiritual theory by Evagrius of Pontus had certain basic presumptions. For them, perfection consisted in the pure intellect enjoying a union of knowledge with the divine. Our bodies are created only as a result of the fall of our intellects. Redemption is achieved through knowledge, and mystical union is expressed in terms of light.

The view developed by Pseudo–Marcarius, an ascetic who probably lived in Mesopotamia in the fourth or fifth century, advocated a psychosomatic understanding of the human person. The soul is not to be separated from the body. Spirituality arises from the sacraments, especially baptism and the eucharist. The heart and not the intellect is the key to spiritual progress. The constant prayer of the heart and what prepares for it should be the ascetic's main preoccupation. His goal is the actual experience of the presence of God and the action of the Holy Spirit. Pseudo–Macarius also described mystical experiences of light, but they are less intellectualist than those of Evagrius.

An alternate world view was taught by Pseudo–Dionysius. While stressing that God is the "Father of Lights" who both enlightens and divinizes us through his image and likeness in which we are imprinted, Pseudo–Dionysius claimed that God is ultimately unknowable. Mystical union involves ignorance and a "cloud of unknowing."

All of these currents of spirituality were to influence the Syriac writers. Evagrius of Pontus had perhaps the greatest impact, especially on those who lived during the period we are studying. His impact is especially evident in the teachings of Philoxenus of Mabboug and Isaac of Nineveh; but even with them Evagrius's influence was tempered by the views of Pseudo–Macarius, among others, and at a later period of those of Pseudo–Dionysius. An example of the last type of synthesis is Simon of Taibutheh.

Even though spiritual teaching seems to cross cultural and geographic lines rather easily and with little resistance, Syriac writers seemed to preserve their native soul and remain faithful to their biblical roots. Thus they present their own authentic witness to the full maturing of Christian faith and love.

# 1

# Early Developments: Ephrem and Aphraat

We have chosen to begin our study of Syriac spirituality with the fourth century. Even though there was great activity in the previous centuries and some works from that period are extant, it was in this century that the various currents of spiritual thought began to take shape. In the Syriac world the fourth century featured the great fathers, St. Ephrem and Aphraat, author of the *Demonstrations*. Another attempt at systematization of spiritual thought in this period was the *Liber Graduum (Book of Steps* or *Book of Degrees)*, which we will discuss in the next chapter.

## Ephrem's Theological Worldview

Ephrem's spiritual teaching is best understood by considering the theological worldview that pervades all of Ephrem's work. It can be summarized by the two themes of God as mystery and the call to become like God (this latter concept Eastern theology was later to call "divinization"). In our relationship with God, from the beginnings of faith and salvation to our consummation in the heavenly banquet, we are involved with a reality that is totally beyond our grasp. God overwhelms us with his presence. But, at no time in our religious experience do we possess God; it is he who possesses us.

God as God is always mystery. The idea of mystery is not defined by saying that we are dealing with things that are beyond our human or intellectual understanding. As the Holy One and Creator, God is mysterious reality itself. He is beyond space and time.

Whatever be our wisdom and knowledge, our only approach to God is through contemplation, in faith and love, in silence. Therefore, only prayer can give birth to theological thought. One can speak of things that pertain to God only if one is brought into divine intimacy through God's grace. Ephrem declares,

> Whenever I have meditated upon You
>   I have acquired a veritable treasure from You;
> Whatever aspect of You I have contemplated,
>   a stream has flowed from You.
> There is no way in which I can contain it:
>   praise to this fountain of Yours.
> Your fountain, Lord, is hidden
>   from the person who does not thirst for You;
> Your treasury seems empty
>   to the person who rejects You.
> Love is the treasurer
>   of Your heavenly treasure store.
>
> (*Hymn on the Faith* 32:2–3)[1]

Yet God has not elected to remain wrapped within his mysterious reality. He has chosen to create, and in the self-same act of creating, he reveals and divinizes. Only the Word is the "Image of the Father" and fully knows the Father. The world is created through the Word. The world in its essence is in the image of God and reveals God. All of creation symbolizes its Creator.

Yet in God's plan, creation would reach its climax and fulfillment in the "Word made flesh." Adam and all humans were created not only in the image of God but in the image of the future Christ, since Christ would one day take on a human nature when creation and humanity were fully prepared for his coming.

Therefore, to be human is to be Christ-like in one's very core. To be human is to have the possibility of, and to be open to, becoming like God. To be human is to be called to an eternal destiny.

Adam's sin and the sinfulness of the human condition in general is due to self-centeredness and the abuse of free will. Sin brings about the distortion of God's image in humans; the accumulation of sin leads to darkness, error, human selfishness and self-destructiveness. However, God, the Compassionate One, in viewing human wretchedness, immediately makes plans for our liberation. He could not allow his image to be lost.

According to God's plan, the world we live in is a "sacramental universe." All of creation waits for and prepares for Christ. Creation and the types or figures in sacred scripture point to and march toward Christ. The universe itself is focussed on and consummated in the Incarnation.

Therefore, by his coming Christ fulfills creation and also com-

pletes revelation. Humans, being finite and feeble, could not
know divinity or grasp its power. God becomes human so that he
can be seen, heard and touched. Divinity humbles itself so that it
can teach, lead and guide us.

Ephrem teaches us that God has hidden many treasures within
his word. Anyone who meditates on scripture is enriched by it.
Ephrem sees God's word as an unquenchable fountain.

However, the God revealed in creation, sacred scripture and the
Incarnation remains unattainable. Ephrem observes,

> Who, Lord, can gaze on Your hiddenness
> Which has come to revelation? Yes, Your obscurity
> has come to manifestation and notification;
> Your concealed Being
> has come out into the open, without limitation.
>
> . . . . . . . . . . . . . . . . .
> Yet who will not fear
> because, even though Your Epiphany is revealed
> and so too Your human birth,
> Your birth from the Father remains unattainable:
> it has baffled all those who investigate it.
>
> (*Hymn on the Faith* 51:2–3)[2]

Christ by his Incarnation restores the divine image and com-
pletes the work of divinization. He who was the only-begotten of
the Father is born a second time in a human condition, so that we
who have been born humanly might be born a second time
divinely.

Christ's redemption is one of healing and restoration and opens
the door to the means of our divinization. The cross of shame
becomes transformed into the "tree of life." Only the creator of life
has the power to defeat sin and death, and to liberate us. Only one
who takes up our human nature subject to death can remove the
fear of death once and for all. Christ defeats death by confronting
death and thus guarantees life and resurrection for all his disciples.

According to Ephrem, the God who creates a world containing
transcending symbols, and who in his public life performs mira-
cles of power, continues his presence through the establishment
of divinizing "mysteries." The Church betrothed at the Jordan
River is wedded to Christ on the Cross. She is born and nourished
by the mysteries of baptism and eucharist that flow from the side
of Christ. She is the new Eve which gives birth through the new

womb of baptism to spiritual and immortal children bearing the
image of the new Adam, who is Christ.

The Holy Spirit is the active principle of divinization. The Spirit
descends on the "mysteries." The presence of the Holy Spirit in
the Church continues the work of transforming all of creation.
The Church is the vehicle whereby new members of Christ are
formed and the source of the sanctifying mysteries. She is the
pilgrim community of faith marching from the paradise of Adam
and Eve to the heavenly paradise.

The mysteries of baptism and eucharist are integral elements in
the process of divinization. Baptism receives its meaning from the
baptism of Christ in the Jordan River and the water flowing from
the side of Christ on the Cross.

The Blessed Virgin Mary is the fulfillment of the Old Testament
types and a symbol of the future Church. Through her virginity
and free assent to the will of the Father, she becomes the model
and example of a fulfilled humanity and its proper relationship
with God. Removing the shame of her ancient mother Eve, and
giving Christ his human body, she becomes the second life-giving
mother of humanity.

## Early Developments: *Bnai* and *Bnat Qyama*

The spirituality of both Ephrem and Aphraat seems to have
been rooted in the gospel message and the life of Christ. The goal
of the spiritual life was to follow Christ in total discipleship. The
foundations of their spirituality were the vows of baptism and the
sacramental life of the eucharist, and this emphasis therefore
entails living the Christian life in community. The ascetics whom
Aphraat and Ephrem advised, as we shall see, presumably lived
within the environs of the local church and possessed a minimum
of exterior organization. Although there existed the temptation to
go to extremes in ascetical practice, the admonitions of Aphraat
and Ephrem were characterized by moderation and common
sense.

An institution that existed in the Syriac world in the early
centuries, and which also sheds light on the nature of Syriac
spirituality, was known as the *Bnai* and *Bnat Qyama* (Sons and
Daughters of the Covenant). It is difficult to determine how exten-
sive or how organized this institution was. However, there is
agreement on its main features. It was an institution that developed within church life proper; it did not entail fleeing from

the world. It was founded on one's baptismal vows and involved an intense commitment to an ascetical life, including a pledge of celibacy. Indigenous Syriac monasticism may well have developed from this institution. On the other hand, it is probable that other more familiar forms of monasticism were imported from Cappadocia and Egypt.

One major source of information on the *Bnai Qyama* is the twenty-three surviving *Demonstrations* of Aphraat written between 336 and 345. Aphraat represents Syriac-speaking Christianity in its purest form, virtually uncontaminated by Greek influence. The *Demonstrations*, if not systematic treatises on spirituality, are at least a manual ordained to practical asceticism. The first ten *Demonstrations*, written in 336–37, give us the ascetical thought of Aphraat.[3] The next twelve followed in 343-44, and the twenty-third in July-August of 345. Because they were written in different times and places, Aphraat's intent shifted from composing a purely didactic treatise on faith and works by which one arrives at perfection to polemical writing against Jews that occurs in the last twelve *Demonstrations*.

In his *Demonstrations* Aphraat uses the word *qyama* seventy-seven times and the Greek loan word *diyatiqi* thirty-five times as a synonym for *qyama*. An argument can be made that Aphraat uses the word so often because it is derived from the root meaning "to stand," thus referring to the "sons and daughters of the covenant" who stand as a sign of their consecrated commitment. *Qyama* can also have the meaning of "covenant" or "pact."[4]

According to Aphraat, those who pledge themselves to this new covenant do not bear an external sign in the way that circumcision signified the old covenant. For him, one should not focus one's attention on matters of the flesh. What was valid for the old covenant must give way to a new circumcision, a circumcision of the heart. The new covenanters must circumcise themselves "in the true Jordan, the baptism of the forgiveness of sins."

George Nedungatt believes that candidates were admitted to the Qyama during a public liturgical service. We are dealing here with a Christian adaptation of the passage on "holy war" in Deuteronomy 20 and of the story of Gideon. Baptism represents the "waters of testing"; one must choose this obligation of a dedicated life freely or withdraw.

In his seventh treatise, *On Penitents*, Aphraat recalls that Gideon chose his select troops in the "test of the water." Only 300 were chosen, while the others withdrew and returned home. Gideon is a model of the candidates who pledged themselves to the Qyama while the others either stayed behind or were advised to rethink their decision.

Aphraat cautions the candidates in his seventh *Demonstration:*

> 'Many are called but few chosen.' Cry and warn the society of God before the Baptism—them I say that have offered themselves for holiness, youths and maidens holy—them shall the herald warn. And they shall say: He whose heart is set on matrimony let him marry before baptism lest he fall in the spiritual contest and be killed. He who is afraid of this sort of battle, let him turn back, lest he should demoralize the fraternity with his panicking. There is nothing to be ashamed of in withdrawing here and now, but later on the one who turns deserter from the fighting line in full armor will incur disgrace before all.

The person who chooses to marry may return at a later time and become a "holy one" [continent].[5]

Murray echoes the above idea when he theorizes that celibate asceticism developed from a very early Judeo-Christian baptismal exhortation of fixed content that involved the following elements: (1) Christ's call to discipleship (Matt. 10:34–9), quoted regularly in a way that fused this passage with Luke 12:49–53; (2) the call to "holy war" drawing on both Old Testament and Pauline passages on ascetical athletics (1 Cor.) and spiritual warfare (Eph. 6); and (3) an exegesis of Joshua's "second circumcision" with "stone swords" (Josh. 5:2), which is related to Christ the "Stone," circumcising hearts with his word, which is sharper than a two-edged sword (Heb. 4:12). Baptism is the new circumcision, as antitype of Joshua, not of the flesh but of the heart. Those who wish to follow Christ in athletic contest and into war are challenged to leave family and possessions. They go down to the "waters of testing," as in the story of Gideon (Judg. 7:5ff), noted above, and submit to the dividing sword, which makes them "single ones": from wife and family, single in heart, and united with the "Only-begotten."[6] Murray observes that Matthew Black has argued that celibacy arose in Judeo-Christianity by an institutionalization of the sexual abstinence required for "holy war."[7]

The type of circumcision of the heart required of the solitary is described in Aphraat's *Demonstration* 11:

> Jesus bar-Nun made the Nation cross over to the land of promise,
> and Jesus our Savior promised the land of life
> to everyone who crossed the "true Jordan"
> and believing, circumcises the foreskin of his heart.

Jesus bar-Nun set up stones for a witness in Israel,
and Jesus our Savior gave Simon the title of Firm Stone *(Kepha)*
and set him as a faithful witness among the Nations . . .
Jesus bar-Nun was called the savior of the Nation,
and Jesus is called the savior of Nations.
Blessed are they who have circumcised their heart of the foreskin
and have been born a second time from the waters of
circumcision . . .[8]

Ephrem's baptismal hymns also refer to Gideon and include reference to Joshua's "second circumcision" of the people with knives of stone. Again, this circumcision of the heart is rendered by Christ the "Stone."

Before ending this section, some questions should be asked. Do the rigorous restrictions outlined above for belonging to the *Bnai* and *Bnat Qyama* imply that there were certain occasions when baptism was reserved only to virgins and committed celibates? It should be safe to say that in common practice baptism was available to all believers, whether they sought to live celibate lives or not. Scholars offer different views regarding the *Qyama*. R. H. Connolly claims that Aphraat cannot be referring to Christians in general. F. C. Burkitt always held the position that baptism was a privilege reserved only for celibates. A. Voobus has suggested that Aphraat was quoting an archaic liturgical formula that was not to be taken literally. A. F. J. Klifn claims that Aphraat spoke only to those already dedicated to virginity who were beginning to waver in their vocation.[9]

### Ihidaya

The call to total commitment by the *Bnai* and *Bnat Qyama* is summarized in the concept of *ihidaya* (single-minded person), which seems to be the term used for consecrated ascetics in early Syriac literature. Aphraat makes clear that the ascetical *ihidaya* (solitary) has a special relationship to the *Ihidaya* (the Only-begotten Son) in *Demonstration* 6: "All the 'single ones' are given joy by the 'Single One' from the bosom of the Father." Ephrem's twentieth *Hymn on the Faith* describes the ascetic's struggle for single-mindedness. This term seems to cover all the consecrated of both sexes, both in virginity and in marriage. It probably has a wider reference than simply those who constitute the *Qyama*.

There are three elements in the meaning of *ihidayuta* (singleness). First, the singleness, which involves leaving family and either not marrying or achieving a degree of withdrawal from the total marriage relationship. This meaning is similar to the *Qyama* idea of becoming "single" by answering Christ's call to leave family. It may be that the emphasis on celibacy had as its aim to attain an inner unity, the opposite of sexual duality.[10] Second, single-mindedness as reflected in the writings of St. Paul and St. James. This meaning is like the *Qyama* in that it requires circumcision of heart and breaking from all that would render us "double-minded" (James 8). Third, a special relationship to Christ, the only-begotten (the *Ihidaya*), whom the consecrated "single-ones" "put on" in a special way. In the context of *qyama*, meaning "to stand," one is called here to "stand up" for Christ.[11]

According to H. J. W. Drijvers, Syriac thought describes Christ as embodying the divine thought and will. Christ manifests the divine will by his obedience unto death through dominating human passions and strivings. The holy person is called to conform to Christ by a similar training of the will. Virginity signifies not a hatred of the body but an imitation of Christ who was an *ihidaya*, that is, only-begotten. One uses free will to control all passions and guide the body. Through the hard exercise of the will, the holy person gains insight into God's saving thought. Asceticism and the acquisition of wisdom are two sides of the imitation of Christ. The desert is the place of trial and the foremost place for the exercise of the will. Drijvers concludes that the goal of the holy person of that time was to imitate Christ by striving to transcend human existence through control of the most fragile part of it, the body.[12]

## The Ecclesiastical Character of the *Qyama*

As we have seen, early asceticism did not necessarily mean going away from society. The purpose of baptism was to bring the Christian into community. The world that was renounced was not the world of cities and people but the domain of evil and infidelity. An early Syriac homily on perfection states, "We ourselves will part from the present world by our piety and sobriety . . . and our spiritual course of life." Ascetics in the Syriac world arose out of the very nature of Christian society, were not a specially labeled class, and were subject to diverse and purely local customs and traditions.[13]

E. Beck observes that one does not find the least indication in Aphraat that groups of ascetics separated from the Christian community to flee to the desert or mountain. The idea of *Bnai Qyama* is closely connected to the sacramental and hierarchical order.[14] In Aphraat, for example, pre-monastic asceticism is tied to the sacrament of baptism. The baptismal hymn attributed to St. Ephrem as the third hymn of Epiphany joins chastity with baptism.

Murray, as mentioned above, considers the idea of total discipleship as the fundamental concept of their ecclesiology. The implication is that the consecrated life is not peripheral but central to the Church. In early Syriac Christianity, the *Qyama* were at the heart or core of the Church. They lived normally and worked in the church community rather than living as anchorites.[15]

The institution of the *Bnai Qyama* assumed different forms as time went on. One description is given by Bishop Rabbula of Edessa (412–35). Rabbula drew up two sets of rules, one for cenobites and another for priests and "sons of the covenant." Whereas the cenobites were required to live regularly in a monastery under a director or superior, a son of the covenant normally lived attached to the Church or with his mother or sister or (in the case of a married man who had decided to practice continence) with his daughter. They were encouraged to live with one another in groups. They assisted at the public celebration of the canonical hours which required the learning of the Psalms.[16] They were to abstain from meat and wine. They observed poverty and were under the charge of the priests. Some served as treasurer of the church. The daughters of the covenant also participated in the Divine Office and practiced abstinence. They assisted the deaconesses of the Church.[17]

## Solitary Ascetics

Besides the *Bnai Qyama*, who were located in the body of the Church, there were the independent ascetics, who resisted all institutionalization and emphasized above all the following of Jesus in his homelessness and poverty.[18] "They lived in the desert or in the mountains like wild animals, totally untouched by any of the semblances of civilization, which was regarded as the work of Satan. They lived in the open, completely exposed to the elements and extremes of heat and cold; they ate roots and wild fruits; their clothing—that is, if they had any at all, and many had not—consisted of straw or leaves tied together; their hair was so shaggy and their nails so long that they resembled birds of prey more than human beings."[19]

Ascetics concentrated on their sins and trespasses and focused their thoughts on judgment day. Their imagination dwelled on the moment of death, the tomb and decay. The meditation practiced by these solitaries was characterized by sadness, mourning, grief and affliction.[20]

Theodoret tells us that the ascetic Jacob, by severely mistreating his body, furthered the development of his soul; his inner eye became pure and was prepared for seeing things hidden to the eyes of ordinary men. Freedom from passions made it possible to see divine mysteries. According to A. Voobus, the Syriac ascetics believed that the Master, in whose name they labored in mortification, repaid them with inspiration, that he directed their inner life and created a particular relationship with them, transforming their natural existence into a spirit-guided life. The result was mystical experience or spiritual seeing. The spirits of the ascetics were thought to be illuminated by higher wisdom and inspired by heavenly mysteries.[21]

## Aphraat and Ephrem on Asceticism

A work of major importance for the history of asceticism in the early Syriac church is Aphraat's sixth *Demonstration,* written in 337. Virginity or continence is essential to the distinctive character of ascetics. It is not the formal cause of sanctity but only the condition of perfect charity and of total indwelling in the soul of the Holy Spirit. The man who has not yet taken a wife is solitary, of one spirit and one thought with his Father. Perfection according to Aphraat consists in the indwelling of the Spirit of Christ, which is in proportion to one's charity; and the condition for its perfection is the renouncing of marriage. We should point out that Aphraat and Ephrem make a distinction between virgins and "holy ones." Virgins refers to those who have never married, and "holy ones" to couples who are married but who have decided to live a life of complete continence.

Aphraat addressed his sixth treatise to the *Bnai Qyama,* both virgins and holy ones. He exhorted his audience first of all to have firm faith because, having come to faith, one is established on the rock that is our Lord Jesus Christ. Without faith, no virtue is of value; reciprocally, faith without works is vain. They were to be zealous in fasting and prayer, fervent in the love of Christ, humble, mild and wise. Their speech should be peaceful and pleasant.

Their thought should be sincere and they should refrain from harmful words.

Ascetics should be modest in dress and avoid feasting. There should be no envy or wrath or speaking about others. Both avarice and begging are to be avoided. They should strive to have no enemies.[22]

Humility or sweetness is the source of intimacy with God, of peace with men, and of intimate joy. As in humility, so fasting is not profitable unless accompanied by purity of heart, that is, the absence of all sin, even by thought, against charity. For Aphraat, fasting applies to the whole range of denial in the spiritual life.[23] One should be freely willing to sacrifice for the sake of love. Therefore, human perfection consists of charity and the spirit of denial that proves it.

Ephrem describes fasting as achieving not only beauty for the soul but brightness to the body. It is a sign of transformation of nature, which prepares for the brightness of the resurrected bodies and renders them similar to the angels. It is a sign of victory over terrestrial desires.

For Ephrem the ascetical ideal is not incompatible with the pastoral and apostolic life. With personal discipline it is possible to observe the principal ascetical virtues in the midst of pastoral and intellectual activities. In his mind asceticism and being in the world are two different conceptions of life, but the ascetic is not necessarily obliged to flee to the desert.[24]

However, it seems that Ephrem considered solitude a special form of the ascetical life. Reflecting on the gospels, Ephrem in his *Hymn on Virginity* (no. 21) declares, "Blessed are you Ephraim, for the Lord of the cities has rested in your faraway city, close to the desert, in the company of solitude, and in a neighborhood full of peace." Ephrem sees in this action of Christ a figure of Christian solitude and an invitation to love the desert.

For Ephrem, virginity is the characteristic virtue of the solitary and his first and principal form of mortification. By the practice of virginity the ascetic becomes not just like the angels but superior to them.

Virginity and holiness (ascribed to those married but living in continence, as noted above) are two complementary charisms. Either way of life, along with faith, renunciation and love, is able to lead to a high degree of perfection. Ephrem speaks of marriage with praise. One must be faithful to the vocation to which he or she has been called by God. We are to live the life for which we are suited in God's plan. Baptism is oriented towards various degrees

of continence. It is not the immersion in a determined state of life
that sanctifies us; it is the manner in which we adapt ourselves to
it and animate it.[25]

The charism of virginity is given only to a minority and is more
easily guarded for the solitary because the desert favors it. Those
who live in the world are more exposed: "The prayer of those who
are far is able to guard those who remain in the village." While
being difficult and perilous, the situation of those in the world is
not without the possibility of a beautiful victory, on condition that
the solitaries help them with their prayer. The contemplative,
who lives for God, lives also for others. Whether one lives in the
world or in the desert, other means available to preserve virginity
are humility, poverty and austerity.[26]

Ephrem in speaking of virginity utilizes marriage vocabulary,
but in a double direction: the virgin espouses not only Christ but
also humanity, since Christ as Groom has given himself for humanity with great love. God requires this love for humanity even
of him who lives in the desert; a passion for the salvation of
humans is essential to the contemplative life.[27]


## Aphraat and Ephrem on Prayer and Salvation

According to S. Brock, Aphraat may have been the earliest
Christian writer to have written a work on prayer in general (other
than on the Lord's Prayer). In the course of his short treatise on
prayer, he offers an intriguing interpretation of Christ's words,
"Enter the chamber and pray to your Father in secret" (Matt. 6:6).
Aphraat comments,

> Why, my beloved, did our Savior teach us saying, "Pray to your
> Father in secret, with the door shut"? I will show you, as far as I am
> capable. He said "Pray to your Father with the door closed." Our
> Lord's words thus tell us "pray in secret in your heart, and shut the
> door." What is the door he says we must shut, if not your mouth? For
> here is the temple in which Christ dwells, just as the Apostle said,
> "You are the temple of the Lord"—for him to enter into your inner self,
> into this house, to cleanse it from everything that is unclean, while the
> door, that is to say, your mouth is closed. If this were not the correct
> explanation, how would you understand the passage? Suppose you
> happened to be in the desert where there was no house and no door,
> would you be unable to pray in secret? Or if you happened to be on
> the top of a mountain, would you not be able to pray? (*Demonstration*
> 4.10. Patrologia Syriaca i.157–60)[28]

For Aphraat, lucidity or purity of heart is not just the prerequisite for "pure prayer"; purity of heart can itself constitute prayer. In the same *Demonstration* Aphraat explains, "Purity of heart constitutes prayer more than do all the prayers that are uttered out aloud, and silence united to a mind that is sincere is better than the loud voice of someone crying out."[29]

Aphraat recalls the many biblical passages in which sacrifices acceptable to God were consumed by fire that descended from heaven. He uses a whole series of biblical examples of sacrifices to illustrate the need for purity of heart if prayer, which has now replaced sacrifice, is to be acceptable to God, insofar as God looks at the interior disposition of the offerer before responding with fire (*Demonstration* 4.2–3). Although Aphraat himself does not go on to connect this fire from heaven directly with the prayer of the heart, he points out that Abel's sacrifice was accepted because of his purity of heart and that this purity of heart, rather than the ensuing sacrifice, was what counted as prayer.

In fact there are occasions, Aphraat points out, when purity of heart must lead to good deeds and not to conscious prayer:

> Be careful, my beloved, that you do not let slip some opportunity of "giving rest" (i.e., giving rest to the weary) to the will of God by saying, "the time for prayer is at hand: I will pray and then act"—and while you are in the process of completing your prayer, that opportunity for "giving rest" will disappear; you will thus be incapacitated from doing the will and "rest" of God, and it will be through your prayer that you will be guilty of sin. Rather, you should effect "the rest" of God, and that will constitute prayer. . . . (*Demonstration* 4.15)[30]

For Aphraat, prayer consists of visiting the sick and taking care of the poor. The ascetic should pray continually day and night and not become discouraged. One prays to implore pardon, to thank the Father in heaven, and to glorify God for his works. Aphraat understood pure prayer in a moral sense; prayer is pure if it is free of sin, especially internal sins against fraternal charity. In summary, "a person should do the will of God, and that constitutes prayer."

Ephrem in his *Letter to Publius* stresses the fact that a person's works and not his state of life are what is important in terms of salvation. In describing judgment day he says,

> I saw there pure virgins whose virginity had been rejected because it had not been adorned with the good oil of excellent works; they

begged their fellow virgins to give them aid, but they got no pity. . . .
And I approached the gate of the kingdom of heaven, and I also saw
there those who did not have the title of virginity, but who were
crowned with victorious deeds, their conduct having filled the place of
virginity. For just as those who had been betrothed to him in body
alone had been rejected, being bare of the clothing of good deeds, so
those whose bodies had been betrothed in chaste marriage, while
their spirit was bound in the love of their Lord, were chosen, being
clothed in love of Him as with a robe, with the desire from Him
permeating all their limbs.[31]

Ephrem also stresses that one must keep one's heart pure and
limpid. He speaks of the "luminous eye" that the Christian should
strive for. For Ephrem Christ is the "Luminous One" and Mary in
contrast to Eve possessed a "luminous eye." Using the image of
the mirror for the quality of our prayer, Ephrem prays,

Let our prayer be a mirror, Lord, placed before your face
then Your fair beauty will be imprinted on its luminous surface.
. . . . . . . . . . . . . . . . . . . . . . . . . .
Let not all sorts of thoughts be imprinted on our prayer;
Let the movements of Your face, Lord, settle upon it, so that, like a
mirror, it may be filled with Your beauty.

(Church 29:9–10)[32]

Ephrem develops this theme further in the use of another
image, namely, that our hearts through internal circumcision can
become a "bridal chamber" where the Creator resides.[33]

In his *Hymn on the Faith* 20, Ephrem examines the relationship
between prayer and faith. Prayer is hidden and internal, whereas
faith is to be expressed. He explains, "Hidden prayer is for the
hidden ear of God, while faith is for the visible ear of humanity. . . . Let prayer wipe clean the murky thoughts, let faith wipe
clean the senses outwardly; and let one such man who is divided
collect himself and become one before You."[34]

Although Aphraat knew of the sweetness of the union with
God and of mystical transports, he did not focus on contemplation.[35] He does speak of the gifts of knowledge and
wisdom. Knowledge is the faculty or the gift of discerning between good and evil. Wisdom, a more subtle faculty, judges
between sincere and only apparent virtues. These and all the
virtues are founded on faith and acquired by humility.[36]

## Disputed Questions

Scholars are not in agreement about the origin of Syriac spirituality. While some view it as native in origin, a contrary position is taken by A. Voobus, who sees a Palestinian Jewish and rigorously ascetic influence on Syriac spirituality.[37] He and others have tried to trace the origins of Syriac spirituality to groups of Judeo-Christians who had emigrated from Palestine. The claim is that these groups were influenced by the Jewish community of Qumran or that strain of Jewish Christianity that was Ebionite and connected to the Essene Jewish milieu. Their asceticism was rigorous, stressing a holy war against the earth and the practice of poverty, abstinence from meat and wine, frequent fasts, privation from sleep, and celibacy. Voobus further claims that among the *Bnai Qyama* there were recluses who had taken a vow of seclusion.

This view is disputed by Jean Gribomont and others who believe that Syriac asceticism developed from a local Judeo-Christianity, influenced by Mesopotamian Judaism and not by migrations coming from Palestine.[38] One can cite St. Ephrem's witness, who described groups of virgins living in the bosom of the community rather than an errant or adventurous asceticism on the mountain. The life of poverty is interpreted to mean one consecrated to prayer and to the apostolate rather than to lucrative work. J. Gribomont concludes that it is such an ascetical group in the heart of the ecclesial church that prepared the way for organized monasticism: "It is here that one ought to look for the most positive contribution of eastern Christians to monastic prehistory, more than in the eccentricities of eaters of herb, anchorites without roof, who have decided to live like savage animals, of stylites and other prodigies of austerity."[39]

Other writers seem to give too much attention to the influence of extremists such as the "encratists," who discouraged marriage.[40] In contrast, both Aphraat and Ephrem spoke clearly in defense of marriage. Ephrem reasoned that marriage and property are goods created by God; we are free either to have them or renounce them. Murray claims, however, that Aphraat and Ephrem saw value in sexual asceticism, either through perpetual virginity or through voluntary abstinence by those already married.[41]

Perhaps these two divergent views, namely moderation and rigorism, can be explained in the observation of R. Murray, who claims that the key inspiration was that of Christian discipleship, which was "taken literally by some as imitation of the poor, homeless and celibate Jesus."[42]

## Conclusion

In this early period of Syriac spirituality, we are at a stage before systematization has taken place, a time prior to lengthy treatises on ascetical practice or the development of theories on the nature of contemplation. This period is characterized by a focus on the scriptures and the call to discipleship. The ultimate goal of Christian living is a singular union with Christ, the *Ihidaya*. But the spiritual life derives its origin and impetus from the sacraments. Therefore, the practice of asceticism and the search for perfection is understood from within the ecclesial community. In their spiritual teaching, Aphraat and Ephrem stress the basic biblical virtues of faith, love, humility, and lucidity or purity of heart. Our prayer to God has meaning only if it is complemented by love toward our neighbor.

# 2

# *Liber Graduum* (Book of Degrees or Steps)

Dating from the fourth century, the *Book of Degrees or Steps* consists of thirty *memre* or homilies. Along with the *Demonstrations* of Aphraat, it is one of the more ancient treatises in Syriac literature that is exclusively consecrated to the spiritual life and that attempts to structure spirituality within a system. According to Aelred Baker, the work may be "related to pseudo-Macarius through the Messalian movement, and it has been suggested that both authors made use of the 'Gospel of Thomas' or books from the same milieu . . . The *Liber Graduum* is well acquainted with ancient apocryphal literature which the author cites frequently."[1] Nevertheless, claims Baker, "the dependence of the *Liber Graduum* on the 'Gospel of Thomas' is wholly unproved by the undoubted existence of rare phrases like 'fasting to the world' in both."[2]

The author of the *Liber Graduum* claims that the evangelical precepts are not addressed to all indiscriminately. One must distinguish between the observance of the "little commandments," which enable the faithful to achieve the state of "justice," and the "great commandments" by which "perfection" is attained. While all are called to perfection, the path is so difficult that only those who have made a "covenant" with the Lord are able to reach it. The perfect are the people who have made this pact and have engaged themselves to live in continence and absolute renouncement. This may be a reference to the "Sons of the Covenant" *(Bnai Qyama)*; the author of the *Liber Graduum* knows this expression and uses it once. Therefore, in the Church there are two classes of faithful, the "just" who observe the commandments relative to justice and the "perfect" who observe the precepts of perfection.

The conduct of the just rests on three fundamental precepts: fasting, prayer and almsgiving. It is directed by the golden rule under both a negative and a positive form: do not do to others what is odious to yourselves; and do to them what you would have them do to you. The just are the "blessed of the Father" to whom the kingdom is promised and of whom Matthew (25:34–40) speaks. The just follow such demands of active charity as feeding the hungry and clothing the naked.[3]

The works of mercy cannot be performed by the "perfect." The perfect obey the precepts of absolute renunciation: they renounce family and marriage to live in continence and celibacy. They leave their homes to lead an errant life, having no place to rest their head. They renounce all their goods, all worldly acquisition, and all commerce with the world. Having nothing, not even a home, they are unable to practice the works of mercy, to give to the poor, to welcome strangers; but they have a great love for all humanity, a love founded on extreme humility, for they believe themselves inferior to all, being the greatest of sinners.

The renunciation of possessions is an expression of an internal self-emptying and leads to hidden prayer of the heart. The *Liber* exhorts,

> Brethren, since we believe that there is a hidden self-emptying of the heart when it leaves the earth and is raised up to heaven, it is right that we should empty ourselves in the body too of our possessions and inheritance. . . . the person who is bound up in our Lord and ponders on him continuously possesses hidden prayer of the heart.[4]

Believing themselves inferior to all, the perfect refuse to judge or condemn anyone and therefore do not accept any charge or authority in the Church. Anyone vested in a dignity should resign from it if he wishes to reach perfection.

The virtues of the perfect are essentially pardon, humility, sweetness. Differing from the just, who are commanded to be distant from sinners because of their weakness, the perfect one is able without danger to break bread not only with sinners but even with pagans, for he is at peace with all. He consecrates his wandering life to prayer, preaching and making peace among people. His prayer is not, like that of the just, limited to certain hours of the day, but is continual. Similarly, he does not fast only on determined days, as do the just, and abstain only from food; his fast is perpetual and universal. The perfect one "fasts from the world," an expression found in the Gospel of Thomas.

The *Liber* also witnesses to the importance of tears in the spiritual life. It explains,

> . . . There are tears that arise from sorrow and there are tears that arise from joy . . . Someone may weep because of his sins—and he

does well to do so, as it is written: Sorrow that is because of God is compunction which turns one to salvation. Others may have conquered sin and moved away from sinful acts to perform good deeds: they weep in joy, out of their love for their Lord who has performed a great act of grace for them.[5]

The author goes on to point out that Our Lord himself shed many tears in prayer. After external sins and faults have been removed, we must offer prayer and supplication and experience anguish in prayer to achieve deliverance from the sin which dwells in the heart.

As time goes on the gift of tears is to be considered a significant element indicating progress in the spiritual life. It is a sign of the sincerity and warmth of the ascetic and a manifestation of the grace of God. Some authors speculate that when perfection is achieved, perhaps only in the next life, tears will cease.

The doctrine of the *Liber Graduum* is described as "pneumatic" or spirit-oriented in the sense that it teaches that a person's spiritual level is proportionate to the measure of Spirit that one has received. The degree of perfection that one has attained depends on the measure of the Spirit that one possesses. Borrowing a Pauline expression, the author claims that the just receive the "pledge of the Spirit." The perfect are those who have received the fullness of the Spirit, the Paraclete.

The "pledge of the Spirit" coexists in the just with what the author calls the "remnants of Satan" or the "remnants of sin." Progress in the spiritual life consists of the increase of the Spirit and the diminishment of the remnants of Satan. Perfection is attained when the latter are reduced to nothing and the Spirit exists no longer as a pledge but is present in fullness.

Between the two states there are a multitude of degrees, according to how much one possesses of the Spirit. There are degrees of justice, and beyond justice, there are degrees of perfection. The author even speaks of a degree that is superior to perfection. The perfect one can reach a point at which he loves more than himself, not only his neighbor but even his enemy and those who persecute him.

The spiritual life thus consists of an indefinite number of degrees. There is, however, a decisive moment when one receives the Paraclete, the Spirit, in plenitude. This event is like a new baptism, the "baptism of fire and the Spirit." By this baptism one enters the celestial church, the church "of the heart" and "of the heights," distinct from the visible church. One is established in the state in which Adam was before the fall, is delivered from all concupiscence and is given access to the "Tree of Life." Although continuing to live on earth, he lives in the Spirit in heavenly dwellings, he knows the entire truth; thus he does not cease to increase in tasting the Spirit until the Lord takes him from the body and establishes him fully in the heavenly Jerusalem.[6]

## The *Liber Graduum* and Messalianism

The claim by the author of the *Liber* that the "remnants of Satan" coexist in the soul with the "pledge of the Spirit" aroused controversy among his contemporaries. Some also took exception to the teaching that the "perfect" transcended the earthly church and so accused the *Liber Graduum* of Messalian tendencies.

The Messalians taught that the demon inhabits humans from their birth; prayer alone is efficacious in chasing out the demon; the Spirit in a sensible fashion comes to inhabit a person after the expulsion of the demon; the abolition of passions in the soul after the coming of the Spirit renders ascetical exercises useless, especially fasting. All knowledge is also useless, because the person who has received the Spirit sees the Trinity itself with the eyes of the body.

There are distinct types of Messalianism. An early group was denounced by Epiphanius and Ephrem about 360 for abuses such as lack of church organization, rebellion against all discipline and absence of an elaborated doctrine. The *Liber* itself refers to tension between ecclesiastical authorities and the perfect, especially in regard to dealings with heretics and pagans.[7] Aelred Baker observes,

> We hear of ecclesiastical sanctions launched by angry bishops at Gangres in 351, against anyone who speaks against marriage or tries to draw married people into a state of virginity. . . . And there is a more serious attack with the same blunt canons at Side in about 370 when a whole movement of Messalian ascetics was condemned.[8]

A completely different type was advocated by the group begun in 380 by Flavian of Antioch and Amphiloqus of Iconium. This group had a clear spiritual doctrine, clear consciousness of the dangers of mystical illusion and a will to remain in the communion of the Church; but they differed from the bishops on where to set priorities. For them "the essential element of relating to Christ and to the communion of the Spirit is situated on the plane of peace of heart and of sanctifying prayer, of which asceticism is the condition and effect. The juridical element of the Church, without being eliminated, is subordinated to the pneumatic."[9]

A. Voobus has challenged the accusation of Messalianism against the *Liber*. He contends that it disagrees with Messalianism at least in the essentials. The author of the *Liber* never affirms that the demon lives substantially in a person. He does not say that prayer alone is efficacious against concupiscence, and he gives equal importance to fasting and to almsgiving.

In particular the author does not hold the Messalian opinion that baptism, the other sacraments and the Church itself are inefficacious. His opinion is clearly defined in Homily 12. Although he admits the existence of an invisible church, the heavenly church or "church on high," of which Jesus is the high priest of the liturgy in which those who have attained perfection participate, he insists that those who wish access to the invisible church must pass through the visible church through baptism, whose value he proclaims, and through its priesthood.

The *Liber* explains:

> By starting from these visible things [the church, altar, and baptism], and provided our bodies become temples and our hearts altars, we might find ourselves in their heavenly counterparts which cannot be seen by eyes of flesh, migrating there and entering in while we are still in this visible church with its priesthood and its ministry acting as fair examples for all those who imitate their vigils, fasting and endurance of our Lord and of those who have preached him. . . . for everything that exists in this church has been established in the likeness of that hidden church. . . .
>
> Accordingly we should not despise the visible church which brings up everyone as children. Nor should we despise this church of the heart, seeing that she strengthens all who are sick. And we should yearn for the church on high, for she makes perfect all the saints.[10]

It is necessary to receive baptism of water in order to receive the "baptism of fire and the spirit" by which one enters the heavenly church. When the perfect one has entered the invisible church, it is not necessary to be separated from the visible church; for it is the same Spirit who ministers to the one and the other.

## Conclusion

The *Liber Graduum* provides a first attempt at systematization of the spiritual life. It already raises some basic questions that we encounter often in the history of spirituality: Is there a real distinction between those who live heroic lives of total discipleship and those who live good but ordinary lives? Can this division be symbolized by a distinction between baptism with water and a baptism of fire and the Spirit? When arriving at higher levels of perfection, does the role of the mysteries (sacraments) become diminished? Does a tension therefore arise between the ascetic and the hierarchical church? Dealing with these issues led to controversy. But we should not forget the dynamic and dedicated audience it was addressing.

# 3

# John the Solitary

In John the Solitary (of Apamea) we see the fruition of early Syriac thought on the spiritual life. The theme of hope, and especially of the world to come, is the hallmark of his work. The scriptures permeate his writings in which he teaches a doctrine of spiritual progress based on biblical anthropology. In addition, he asserts, it is baptism and the sacraments that initiate and nourish the spiritual life.

John the Solitary was a Syrian monk of the fifth century. His works were addressed to his companions in the solitary life, who consulted him on questions of theology or the spiritual life. Indications in the *Chronicle* of Michael the Syrian support the conclusion that John the Solitary lived in the second half of the fifth century and, according to all appearances, around the environs of Apamea.[1] There is some speculation that John may have been associated with the Monastery of St. Maron.

Except for a single citation from Ignatius of Antioch, John cites only the scriptures. He reveals a good knowledge of Greek philosophy and a marked interest in medicine. Irenée Hausherr believed that he could link John's spirituality of hope to Ignatius of Antioch and Ephrem and his doctrine of baptism to Mark the Hermit.

John's writings influenced later Syriac monastic literature. Isaac of Nineveh (seventh century) cites John only once; but he depends on his philosophy, his insistence on hope, and his tripartite division of the spiritual life into body, soul and spirit. Joseph Hazzaya (eighth century) was also influenced by John.

The name of John the Solitary became suspect among his contemporaries by reason of accusations of gnosticism brought against his doctrine. He himself distinguishes his thinking from the teachings of the Valentinians, a gnostic sect. As noted above, his thought is dominated by the idea of hope in the life of the world to come; this fundamental principle dominates his interpretation of the whole economy of salvation and of the nature of the spiritual life. It is from these two perspectives—history of salvation and the life of the individual soul—that he teaches his spirituality of hope.


## History of Salvation

According to John the Solitary, from the moment of their creation humans are oriented toward hope: "Man has been placed in this world in the expectation of the world to come." The human person comes to discover the transcendent aspirations of his soul, which direct him to the hope of something which is beyond this world; this hope is confirmed by the traces of God in the wisdom and beauty of creation. The soul appreciating the wisdom of God as discovered in the appearances of the world should curb the ingrained passions of the body, which are directed only to the visible. Instead, the body seduces the soul and renders it an accomplice to its worldly desires, and so the soul's vision of God throughout creation becomes obscured.

It is to remedy this situation that God has inaugurated a second plan, according to which he has chosen to manifest himself to the humble people of Israel and through them to all people. By the law and by his promises, by the experience of salutary trials and divine protection, God has not ceased to uncover for man another hope. Man can be liberated from error and corruption insofar as the Lord himself is revealed as the true "day" to awaken humans from their sleep, to lead them to God and to show them anew the light, whose sight they have lost. By coming into the world, Christ brings the definitive revelation of hope. It is the incarnation of a truth which has been prefigured throughout history in creation and the providential intervention of God; but human beings have not understood.[2]

This revelation of hope is made by Christ's death and resurrection: "In resurrecting from the dead in the glory of the Father, he wishes to show us and reveal to us, our proper hope, our resurrection and our true life." This is the underlying basis of the theology of John the Solitary. Christ realizes in a unique and perfect fashion the spiritual life to come, beyond the passions and the purification of the soul. All those who rise from the dead will resemble him in the world to come.

At the same time, the life of Christ in the midst of the world enables us to see our situation and our task. Christ's temptations indicate the combat in which humans are engaged with the powers of evil; his crucifixion shows how we are tied by our passions and ought to crucify them in order to be tied to Christ; his death reveals the state of corruption of humanity and the necessity for us to die to this world so that we may live in Christ.

Christ is the author of our faith because we have received from him the knowledge of the new world. Christ is the consummation because in him we discover the fullness of our hope.[3]

## Resurrection through Baptism

Through the gift of baptism, Christ communicates to us in actuality what he has revealed. In the same way that the death and resurrection of Christ mark the end of this life and the beginning of the new life, so baptism is, in the soul, the frontier between servitude to sin or slavery under the law and the spiritual liberty of the gospel that makes people sons and daughters of God. The empire of death and demonic powers that perpetuate humanity in a state of illusion are abolished; the soul, rendered invisible to Satan, enjoys the community of angels and eternal life.[4]

With baptism, the new man receives an increase of knowledge and is directed to the heavenly Jerusalem. Through the second birth of baptism, Christ engenders in us both the grace and the hope of new life. Baptism is not only forgiveness of sins but also communion with God. Its principal effect is to make us children of God so that we may enjoy the liberty of the new life. For those who are baptized, it is not the law that is teacher but the baptismal mystery, which becomes our master to guide us by the exercise of knowledge toward the truth that will manifest itself.[5]

There are two stages of resurrection, one at baptism that introduces us to spirituality, and the second that ushers the body into eternity. If a person remains without fault after baptism, he is already in a new life, except he has not yet achieved this state in knowledge. Just as Jeremiah was consecrated prophet in his mother's womb but his vocation appeared only later, so by baptism we are sanctified for a future glory; but its full manifestation will take place only in the world to come. Here we have a partial anticipation of the contemplation proper to the future life, a presentiment of good to come. The future glory is as transparent as dawn to the eyes of faith.

With the resurrection of the body, God will give us true knowledge; we will then be new persons without sin or carnal thought. The present world is made of inert elements that manifest the wisdom of God. On earth we know by empirical knowledge, painfully gotten; the saints know God by an interior perception without intermediary.[6]

## Spiritual Progress

For John the aim of the Christian life is to bring into actuality, as far as is possible, the new life of resurrection inaugurated by Christ, the hope and pledge of which has been given to each Christian at baptism. In his *Dialogue on the Soul,* John divides the spiritual life into three "orders" which he believes to be mentioned in scripture (see 1 Cor. 3): those who live by the flesh (somatics), by the soul (psychics), and by the spirit (pneumatics). He understands by these orders not three natures or temperaments but three orientations or different passions of the soul. The predominance of one or the other indicates at what stage one is in the spiritual life. The highest degree pertains not to life in this world but to that of the resurrection which follows. Therefore, the highest constant level that one can attain in this world is that integrity of the soul which is intermediate between virtuous conduct in the present life and spiritual understanding in the future life. Hope remains the fundamental principle of the whole spiritual life; it determines its nature and leads man beyond all obstacles to the final end.[7]

### CORPOREAL OR SOMATIC STAGE

Corporality is the condition in which humanity exists before experiencing hope. When one is an infant, one's regard is limited to the visible world. In corporeal man the order wished by God, and in virtue of which the soul would dominate the body and lead it to the knowledge of God, has been completely reversed. The body is entirely governed by passions, and because of them the soul is disfigured by evil thoughts.[8]

The corporeal man is the one who refuses to practice exterior works of asceticism and whose tendency is to bad thoughts. He is still a "slave of sin." Granted the ability to love by nature, his love is unstable. He seeks after his body and its material joys. He desires worldly power and riches.[9]

His relationship with God, who is represented in an anthropomorphic manner, is self-seeking and superficial. He experiences neither fear nor repentance in God's presence, and mundane interests occupy his thoughts even in time of prayer. He does not meditate on the word of God. In these conditions, the corporeal man is incapable of knowing the mystery of God.[10]

But hope in the world to come permits a person to deliver himself from his passions and from his love for the visible world. This is the heart of the doctrine of John: "Apply yourself to understand the future hope, and you will master your passions." When the soul is awakened and doubts itself, the combat is able to begin. Corporeal man then has access to the next level, that of the soul.[11]

One goes from fear to charity by liberating oneself from the servitude of the passions. Prayer is necessary to obtain victory and interior peace.

### LIVING ACCORDING TO THE SOUL (PSYCHIC STAGE)

He who turns from his body and fulfills the activity of the soul by virtuous actions is called "psychic" (Greek word for "soul"). But the psychic man is still an "exterior man"; he understands only the "visible" things. For this reason he is not able to know how to judge spiritually.

The psychic stage is a transition between the quasi-animal submission to the body, which characterizes the somatic stage, and the perfect spirituality of the angels, which pertains to the future world. The constant illusion of psychic man is that the level of virtue or of wisdom to which he has arrived constitutes perfection; in this persuasion, he takes pride in his progress and condemns others.[12]

Thus, in this stage, charity is not yet completely genuine; for true love, according to John, "is not acquired by the work of the body, but by comprehension of the mysteries"; yet psychic man still has not attained this level.[13] Figures and allegories are the vehicles that make known to him the existence of mysteries. Reality remains in the new world.[14]

The psychic level consists of obedience to the commandments and the practice of virtue. It involves asceticism, fasting, vigil, manual labor. Prayer is the principal manifestation of the psychic state, but at this stage it is neither pure nor continual. There are still distractions and memories of one's former life. There is the need for silence and quiet.[15] One must detach oneself from all that holds the soul captive, such as earthly goods and too close an attachment to relatives and friends. The battle is against external and internal temptations. The fear of God invades the soul, and so this stage is marked by the gift of tears.

The combat is long and painful: it requires numerous transformations in the interior man. Hope is the force which guides and carries one beyond the attractions of the visible world and its hidden illusions.

STAGE OF THE SPIRIT (PNEUMATIC STAGE)

John describes this level as a "mystery which is not able to be defined." Passions have been purified from the interior; man has passed beyond the exercise of virtue and of human wisdom to a particular state which is of the spiritual order: a communion with God through the revelation of his mystery.

The life of the pneumatic (Greek for "spirit") person presupposes total detachment from the body and from the world. "After man has risen from the passions, he is judged worthy to enter into the region of life which is the love of God, where he receives in revelation the vision of the mysteries; when he has arrived to the peace of love, his soul exalts in quietude, in the shelter from interior combats."[16]

Other signs of the spiritual level are largeness of spirit and generosity of heart with solicitude for all people, both just and sinners. The spiritual person is dominated continually by admiration for the depth of the wisdom of God and by the idea that this life is infinitely inferior to the future mystery.[17] Also at this stage there are no more tears, since the angels do not weep.

The spiritual person is turned totally toward God. "He is no longer in conflict with Satan because his conduct is hidden to all but God alone"; he is no longer a slave to anyone who imposes orders "but a well-beloved son, freed from all that is of this world."[18]

Having arrived at "purity of soul," man attains, in his soul and in his body, "luminosity or transparence of soul," which permits him to "perceive the knowledge of mysteries of the other world." There are no more obstacles, neither of the psychological order nor of the intellectual order, to separate him from "concentration in God" or to prevent him from acquiring an "intellect united to God by the knowledge of his mysteries."[19]

In his work *Dialogue on the Soul,* John gives a detailed description of the way purity of soul is attained and of its effects. After self-emptying of the love of money and the love of praise, one practices humility, forbearance and serenity and strives for perfect love of God and of human beings.

> For it is by these things that a person approaches purity of soul, which is the sum of the entire way of life which God bade human beings to follow during this life. For all his commandments bring a person as far as transparency of soul. Now once he has done battle and overcome all the evil passions, and stands in purity of mind, a person leaves the entire way of life commanded by God in this life, and henceforth he begins to enter in from transparency of soul to the way of life of the New Person. No longer is he a servant subject to a law, but a beloved son who has been liberated from everything that belongs to this world. He begins to become a sharer in the mystery of God.[20]

However, in the strict sense, only Christ has attained this condition on earth. It is true that, for the man who has passed the integrity of the soul, "God begins to give him here below something of the charisms to come, in the measure that he is capable to receive them in this life." But, although man sees in his soul "the exquisite beauty of the mysteries of God," he sees them only under a corporeal form as long as he is on the earth.

The future glory appears already as the dawn to the eyes of faith. The mystique of John of Apamea consists of living eternity in time. Reality exists only after the second resurrection.[21]

## John on Prayer

John deals with two types of prayer, the vocal prayer of the psychic man, which should strive to be continual; and interior silent prayer, which the "spiritual" person experiences and which never lasts long in this life.

According to Sebastian Brock, behind John's teaching on prayer is his understanding of the Incarnation. For him, the word of God springs from silence. He puts on the body as the human word puts on voice. "God's silence spoke with our voice so that we might hear." Humans are called to reverse the process and go from the world of utterance to the world of silence. John distinguishes five types of silence: silence of the tongue, of the whole body, of the soul, of the mind and of the spirit. "The silence of the spirit is when the mind ceases even from stirrings caused by created spiritual beings and all its movements are stirred solely by

Being, at the wondrous awe of the silence which surrounds Being."[22]

In other writings, John distinguishes between the "world of the word," which is the spiritual realm, and the "world of the voice," which is our earthly world. In the invisible world there is no voice, for not even voice can utter its mystery. John asks, "When shall I become word, in an awareness of hidden things, when shall I be raised up to silence, to something which neither voice nor word can bring?"[23]

In his treatise *On Prayer* John advises that our prayer should be in spirit because God is Spirit. Spiritual prayer is more interior than the tongue or vocal words. "When someone prays this kind of prayer he has sunk deeper than all speech, and he stands where spiritual beings and angels are to be found. Like them he utters 'holy' without any words."[24]

However, to arrive at interior prayer takes much preparation. As mentioned above, a person must pray externally and continually for a long period. He must chant the psalms, fast, abstain and devote himself to ascetical works. The soul must be filled with humility and the remembrance of God.

John advises the reader that even the internal word is of no value unless it is embodied in our actions. Word must become deed, so that the world may see you "to be a man of God."[25]


## Conclusion

With John the Solitary we see a systematic spirituality. While his tripartite division of corporeal, psychic and pneumatic has some analogy to spiritual masters of other traditions, his synthesis developed from biblical roots and from the Syriac world view. The life, teaching, death and resurrection of Christ are the model par excellence for all those seeking the spiritual life. From the Syriac tradition John emphasizes a symbolic view of creation and concludes therefore that genuine spirituality is a sacramental spirituality. Reflecting the Syriac liturgy, he proclaims the constant theme of hope and its eschatological ramifications. John's psychology of the spiritual life is based on biblical anthropology and not on extraneous sources. In John the Solitary we see a master of the spiritual life who has fully integrated all his indigenous resources.

# 4

# Evagrius of Pontus

Evagrius of Pontus represents a systematic synthesis of Neo–Platonic thought and the writings of the Egyptian desert fathers. While he was not of the Syriac tradition, his system and teachings had a profound and long-lasting impact on spiritual thought and subsequently influenced many of the major spiritual writers of the Syriac world. It is for this reason that we are including a chapter on his thought.

Evagrius was born in Pontus around 345. He was originally a student of St. Basil of Caesarea and turned to St. Gregory Nazienzen after the death of Basil. Subsequently he withdrew from Constantinople and by 383 established himself in the Egyptian desert, where he spent the rest of his life. He died in 399. His writings on asceticism and spirituality reflected many of the teachings of the desert fathers. Evagrius sought to order these teachings into a developed system.

## His Theology

In his worldview and theology, Evagrius was very much influenced by Neo–Platonic thought and the writings of Origen. Evagrius taught that a nonmaterial universe preceded the present created world. From eternity God had created "pure intellects" or "rational beings" whose purpose was to know God and be united with him without distinction.

The true nature of the mind was to be fixed on God. Any distraction can lead to evil. However, these spiritual beings sinned through negligence and therefore moved away from God. God in his mercy performed a second creation in which fallen intellects were given bodies and thus the means to work their way back through stages of knowledge. By means of various levels of contemplation, the body becomes more and more spiritual.

For Evagrius, therefore, our souls are fallen intellects. Our bodies are not essential to us, since our nature is to be purely intellectual. Our perfection is of the intellectual order and consists ultimately of a complete union of knowledge with the Holy Trinity. Even charity is subordinated to the knowledge of God.

The humanity of Christ was also originally an intellect but did not sin and so remained united with the Divine. Christ voluntarily assumed a body to save humans through knowledge. Humans must purify their intellects through stages of contemplation. When we have reached complete purification, we will achieve union with the Godhead through knowledge. At that point, our bodies will no longer be necessary.


## Ascetical and Spiritual Teaching

In developing a framework for progress in spirituality, Evagrius adopts the three fundamental stages outlined by Origen. Origen divided the spiritual life into the stage of *praktiké* or action, in which one struggles to overcome the passions and arrive at *apatheia* or the state of "passionlessness"; the stage of *gnosis* or *theoria*, which involves the contemplation of both sensible and intellectual creation; and *theologia*, or the contemplation of the Trinity.

### STAGE OF *PRAKTIKÉ* OR ACTION

Evagrius claims that it is impossible to achieve contemplation without *apatheia*, or passionlessness. Referring to the vision of Moses in Exodus, he says that if the soul is to perceive the place of God within itself, it must arise above all thoughts and concerns and detach itself from the passions which tie it to sensible things.[1]

At this stage one must observe the commandments and practice the virtues of faith, temperance, prudence, patience, hope and fear of the Lord. The goal is to subdue the passions so as to reach a state of *apatheia*, at which point the fire of the passions is totally diminished. And *apatheia* engenders charity. However, *apatheia* does not completely exclude the attacks of the demons, since no stage of the spiritual life is exempt from temptations.

In dealing with the passions Evagrius lists eight major vices that must be overcome: gluttony, fornication, avarice, sadness, anger, discouragement or *acedia*,[2] vainglory and pride. This listing is the origin of what later became known as the seven capital sins in the West. Regarding each sin, Evagrius presents a detailed analysis and appropriate remedies. A sign that one is approaching the state of *apatheia* is that one is no longer bothered not only by external objects but even by memories of them.[3]

## STAGE OF *GNOSIS* OR *THEORIA*

The second stage of spiritual progress involves contemplation.[4] There are two major divisions in this stage: contemplation of material things and the contemplation of rational or noncorporeal beings. The intellect is called to ascend toward God by a progressive purification. The goal is to return to its pristine condition of divine contemplation.

In the contemplation of material things, one studies not only their natures but their very "reasons" *(logoi)* for being according to God's wisdom, reasons which are implanted in creatures and which tend toward God. In a similar way, when one contemplates the sacred scriptures, the goal is to understand the reasons that the symbols embody. One must distinguish between the letter and the spirit of scripture. True contemplation is possible when the purified intellect comes to understand the proper role of each creature in God's universal plan.[5]

The contemplation of noncorporeal beings is a participation in the knowledge of the angels. In fact, some have distinguished five categories of *theoria* or contemplation in Evagrius. The highest is *theologia* or the contemplation of the Holy Trinity. Below it are the contemplation of noncorporeal and corporeal beings. The lowest levels are the *theoria* of God's judgment and of his providence. However, as time went on, spiritual writers seemed to bypass the middle levels of contemplation and to go directly from the level of *praxis* to the level of contemplation of the Trinity. Perhaps the contemplation regarding the inner meanings of creatures enjoyed its greatest popularity as a tool in seeking the spiritual sense of scripture.[6]

## STAGE OF *THEOLOGIA* OR CONTEMPLATION OF THE HOLY TRINITY

The highest level of contemplation is of the Holy Trinity. For Evagrius this final stage is quite different from those before it. It is simple, immaterial, beyond all forms and concepts. Pure prayer is above thoughts and entails the suppression of thoughts. It is knowledge involving the essence of the soul. Where previous contemplations entailed activity, progress and falling back, the contemplation of the Trinity is marked by peace and repose. It is not within our power but must be freely granted by God. This contemplation becomes possible only if the light of the Trinity lifts the soul at the time of prayer and the soul becomes filled with this light.

This highest contemplation requires the total nakedness of the intellect (*nous gymnos* in Greek), which has returned to its pristine origin where it can mirror again the image of God. Now, after successive purifications, it has recovered its unity with the Divine. Evagrius describes it as seeing "the place of God." While stating that God is inaccessible in himself, Evagrius uses phrases such as "to see God" and "the vision of God." In his work *Praktikos*, Evagrius makes reference to the vision of Moses in the Book of Exodus (Septuagint, Ch. 24:9–11) and describes the mind removing its veil, experiencing its proper state in prayer as sapphire, which is the biblical description of the place of God on Mount Sinai. Perhaps he is claiming that one sees God indirectly in the beauty of the deified soul, which is now the purified image of God.[7]

Because of his Origenist background, Evagrius is considered an advocate of a mysticism of light. The ultimate goal of prayer and contemplation is perfect knowledge; this knowledge reaches its conclusion in an ecstatic union with the Trinity. This theory is in contrast to a mysticism of darkness, among whose advocates are Gregory of Nyssa and Pseudo–Dionysius. For these spiritual masters, the goal of the intellect is to surrender itself ultimately, to reach a level of ignorance which is above any human knowledge. The intellect ceases to function, and no further human understanding *(theoria)* is possible. One has arrived at a region of darkness which contains the presence of the Divine.

## Conclusion

One approach in developing a program for the spiritual life is to focus on the psychology of the soul, its sinful condition, and its growth and development. Evagrius chose this option; and with his desert experience and the writings of the desert fathers, he was able to construct an in-depth understanding and method for the progress of the soul. Evagrius's focus on the soul was no doubt the result of his acceptance of the Origenist and Neo–Platonic worldview. For the same reason, we also understand his stress on the intellect and on knowledge as the goal of the spiritual life.

While these emphases on the part of Evagrius could lead to

distortions, to a depreciation of the significance of the body, and perhaps to a downplaying of the role of the sacraments in the spiritual life, there is no doubt that the basic approach of Evagrius had a great impact on the fundamental theory of Christian spirituality and a strong influence on Syriac writers. We can see his direct effect on such renowned Syriac writers as Philoxenus of Mabboug, Isaac of Nineveh and Joseph Hazzaya. The one who took his teachings and especially their Origenist elements to their most extreme conclusion was Stephen Bar Sudaili. We describe the latter's teachings in an appendix to this work.

# 5

# Philoxenus of Mabboug

Philoxenus of Mabboug represents a transitional point in both Syriac theology and spirituality. In Philoxenus we have a person who was rooted in the Syriac world but was also influenced by Greek culture. He wrote on a wide range of theological subjects.

In the field of spirituality Philoxenus, although still coming out of the Syriac world, is clearly a disciple of Evagrius of Pontus. The evangelical and practical asceticism of Aphraat and Ephrem are now giving way, in Philoxenus, to an intellectualist stress. Evagrius's doctrine on spirituality, heavily influenced by the teachings of Origen, becomes the predominant teaching.[1]

Philoxenus was born in the fifth century in Iraq and studied at Edessa. He was made bishop of Mabboug in 485. Because of his opposition to the Council of Chalcedon, he was eventually deposed and sent into exile, where he died in 523. In addition to his commentary on scripture and his writings on theological issues, Philoxenus wrote extensively about the spiritual life, much in the form of letters.[2]

The Evagrian influence is readily seen in the writings of Philoxenus. For example, in his work on the Trinity and Incarnation, Philoxenus speaks of asceticism as a way to arrive at *gnosis* (knowledge). Praxis consists in obeying the commandments. But there is possible a knowledge of natures that is not acquired by study and consists in knowing the inherent "reasons" of things. The intellect is able to contemplate its proper nature. Charity is prior to *gnosis*, and the goal of *gnosis* is "theology." All these themes are found in Evagrius.[3]

Perhaps the most extreme case of Evagrian Origenism is to be found in the writings of Stephen Bar Sudaili (ca. 500) in his *Book of the Holy Hierotheos* (See appendix). Philoxenus attacks Sudaili's work as "pantheistic doctrine of consubstantiality of God and of the material universe, the redemption of all which exists by assimilation with the divine principle."[4]

## Philoxenus's Worldview

Before reviewing the spiritual teachings of Philoxenus, it is helpful to consider his theological worldview. Philoxenus accepts the biblical teaching on the creation of the universe and humans: creation came into existence by the Word of God. While the universe serves as a "divine pedagogy," as a result of sin it is difficult for humans to understand spiritual matters beyond sensible appearance; the universe has to be deciphered. Humans are created by love and called to reciprocate the love of their Creator. Because of sin, humans are deprived of the plenitude of freedom and submit to the passions, ignorance, error, the powers of evil and death. The tendency to disorder is not sin but the "door to sin."

According to Philoxenus, God became human so that humans might become God. The role of the Incarnate Word is to give divine life and to restore the bond of filiation and love destroyed by sin. As the new Adam, Christ has restored human nature. With the Incarnation, we have already recovered in some way our original state.

The redemptive work of Christ results in the divinization of the new man and woman. New creation through the humanity of the Word gives new possibilities to human nature to find again the necessary health to reach God by contemplation after having lived a moral ascetical life.

It is through baptism that Christians are born as new and spiritual human beings. A moral and contemplative life is the fulfillment of the potentiality contained in baptism. Through charity, one becomes the seer of all things spiritual.[5]

## Spiritual Teachings

Paul Harb tells us that Philoxenus's doctrine termed *la-hasusuta* in Syriac has as its immediate source Evagrius's doctrine of *apatheia*. For Evagrius, as we have seen, the spiritual life consists of *praktiké, physiké* and *theologia*. The order of these three steps is necessary; each prepares for what follows. The *praktiké* consists in the ascetical life, the exercise of the virtues of faith, fear of God, abstinence *(enkrateia)*, perseverance and hope. The ascetic achieves *apatheia* only at the term of the *praktiké*, which should be practiced according to the indicated order, since the virtues are tied one to the other in an ascending logic of purifying until impassibility is reached.

For Philoxenus also, the exercise of the Christian life is a purification of the intellect beginning in faith and ending in contemplation. In addition, Philoxenus adopts Evagrius's triple division of *theoria*, namely, the contemplation of "composed natures," that is, nonrational and corporeal creatures; the contemplation of "natures not composed," that is, rational and spiritual beings; and the contemplation of the "uncreated nature," that is, the Trinity. Also like Evagrius, Philoxenus speaks of the contemplation of Divine Providence, judgment, sacred scripture and the Holy Mysteries.[6]

## Faith and the Commandments

Faith is the point of departure. Nothing can be done that is real and solid in the moral life without faith. Faith enables us to realize in practice what was accomplished mystically in us by baptism. With faith we build our moral life "on the rock" of the new man born in baptism.[7]

Upon faith is built the fear of God. From the latter proceeds *enkrateia*, the fundamental ascetical virtue, of which continence is only a particular form. *Enkrateia* consists of the resistance to all impulses of the passions. By the exercise of patience, which is the next virtue, we not only resist the attraction of pleasure but bear what is painful. Patience gives birth to hope, which is the awaiting of true goods. The result is *apatheia* (passionlessness), which engenders *agapé* (charity).

This order develops, according to the *Letter to Patricius*, by the keeping of the commandments. Philoxenus writes,

> Whoever says that his soul does not yet have spiritual liberty because he has not overcome the passions, how can he say that his soul loves to love God? It is impossible that the love of God moves in the soul, if it has not overcome its passions . . . There is no way then to be lover without observing the commandments. And if one does not observe all the commandments, not only has one not arrived at contemplation which is union with Christ, one will not even inherit life.[8]

The goal of the divine commandments is to lead us to the state of first innocence. They are the only means for overcoming the maladies of the soul. The virtue of charity requires the health of the soul, which can only be achieved by asceticism.[9]

The soul is composed of three parts, the rational, the concupiscible and the irascible. It is only when these three parts are
"harmoniously reunited" that they act according to the natural
strength of each. However, according to Philoxenus it is impassibility which realizes this harmony. In each of these parts of
the soul reside the virtues which are proper to it: the rational—
intelligence and wisdom to "examine the knowledge which is in
the natures"; the concupiscible—charity "aspiring to union of
spiritual things"; and the irascible—courage and the power to
combat vices.[10]

The body, according to Philoxenus, enjoys an important role in
the acquisition of *la-hasusuta*. It is an indispensable instrument for
ascetic purification. Although its nature is from below, it has been
created not to desire things from below but to desire spiritual
things. If it devotes itself to works, it will constitute with the soul
a virtuous body, worthy of respect.

For Philoxenus, *la-hasusuta* is a state which is realized progressively. At the end of his course, the true ascetic acquires
"knowledge," *ida'ata*. This knowledge fortifies the intellect and
strengthens it in impassibility. At this stage the monk acquires the
"liberty of the spiritual ones" and becomes "similar to the angels."
His soul is no longer "questioning" but "seeing."

*La-hasusuta* is not an end in itself. It constitutes the end of praxis
but has in view the acquisition of *gnosis*, or "spiritual knowledge,"
which by the mediation of *agapé* leads to contemplation.[11]

Only after Philoxenus has spoken about faith, simplicity, fear of
God, detachment and abstinence, only after having cautioned at
length about the importance of purification by keeping the commandments and Christian asceticism, does he speak of the new
man, impassible and capable of love, of visions and of contemplation (*theoria*) of God.

## The Stage of Perfection

Philoxenus affirms the idea that once free of the passions and
liberated from all "malice," the soul acquires "purity," defined as
being the "kingdom of the soul." It recovers its "first health" and
becomes able not only to desire spiritual things ordained to its
immaterial nature but also to surpass its condition and to desire
things which are "above its nature." "While the intellect is renewed and the heart sanctified, all movements of desire which
survive in it, are moved according to the nature of the new

spiritual world in which it enters."[12] For, having arrived at this stage, the "apathetic" person is born anew. He casts off the former world and attains divine things. Another world receives him.

> The love of divine things is stirred in the intellect. It desires communion with the holy angels, and the revelation of the mysteries of spiritual science; the intellect becomes sensible to the spiritual knowledge of beings; and then the dawn of contemplation relative to the mysteries of the Trinity rises in the mysteries of the adorable Economy of God in our favor. And then it is united to the plentitude of the knowledge of hope of the future.[13]

Evagrius presents charity as the "door of knowledge." Philoxenus takes this notion and considers charity as the "door" of contemplation. When the intellect enters this door, it will march "sovereignly" in the ways of contemplation, "without any obstacle being made to it." Besides, charity is considered as "the first contemplation of the Trinity." In its turn, it strengthens contemplation, which becomes as if "implanted in nature," and the monk becomes "naturally" the "seer" of all spiritual things.[14]

Holiness is different from contemplation, since sanctity is able to exist without contemplation. Contemplation depends on God alone. Contemplation obtained by a means other than virtue is subject to illusion. It is false if it leads to corporeal visions. (In this way, Philoxenus stands against the Messalians.)[15]

Faith becomes "spiritual wisdom" in the measure of the charity and the "purity of intellect" that the believer realizes in himself. This spiritual wisdom is a radically simple and immediate intuition that cannot be expressed in words and is accomplished without the mediation of mental images. Contemplation operates by a direct contact between the pure intellect, which "looks in itself," and the knowledge of the Holy Spirit, who is imprinted there.[16]

In an *Excerpt on Prayer*, Philoxenus declares,

> The converse of the Holy Spirit (which dwells within us) with God is the aim of all ascetic labours, and the end of the path of righteousness: this is the ministry of the company of Gabriel and Michael. For prayer, I would say, is not psalmody consisting of verses, or songs and hymns: these just serve as the letters and syllables for prayer's authoritative form of reading. Until we become aware that within us there lives the "spiritual person," along with all his limbs—that is to say, what we become in baptism—battle against that "old person" whom Christ put to death on his Cross, will not be stilled within us.[17]

Thomas Spidlik observes that it seems that the Syrian authors understood ecstasy as the posture of a soul perfectly detached from distractions; it is a recompense for moral purity resulting from the victory over the passions.[18]

Thus, we see that Philoxenus of Mabboug was able to introduce the doctrine of Evagrius into a Syriac milieu. Apparently, Evagrius's analysis of the soul and his method of purification struck a universal chord. With such writers as Philoxenus Syriac spirituality entered a new phase, which was to reach its culmination in the doctrine of Isaac of Nineveh and his seventh-century contemporaries.

# 6

# Pseudo–Dionysius the Areopagite

Although the writings bear the name of Dionysius the Areopagite, the actual author wrote between 480–520, was probably a monk as well as a Syrian, and wrote in Greek. The first explicit quotation from Dionysius was recorded at a meeting of bishops in Constantinople in 533.

Thanks to the commentaries of Maximus the Confessor (d. 662), the Dionysian writings enjoyed an uncontested authority in the theological tradition of the East as well as an impact on the West. Dionysius is frequently cited by St. Thomas Aquinas. His treatises on angels, on the hierarchy, and his liturgical writings had a broad influence. But regarding Maximus the Confessor himself, I. Hausherr claims that despite his exegesis of Dionysius he was before all else a disciple of the Alexandrians and Evagrius. Also, Dionysius seems to have arrived too late to an epoch in which eastern mystical doctrine had already received its classic form. The essential themes of eastern spirituality—deification, darkness, ecstasy—were known, used and commented upon before Dionysius.

Furthermore, the Dionysian theological speculations do not appear to have especially attracted the spiritual writer; and no one could be found who was capable of popularizing his abstruse theories, which were exposed in a very obscure style.[1] However, select Dionysian themes in philosophy, theology, exegesis and liturgy were commented upon at length by eastern writers.

André Rayez claims that in the East, Dionysius the theologian, rather than the mystical writer, had the greater influence. He becomes prominent in the christological and trinitarian controversies. He also is cited in matters of liturgy and sacraments. The spiritual masters of the East were the ascetics, not the theoreticians. Speculation, when it did occur, was along traditional lines.[2]

Knowledge of Dionysius's works spread very soon in Syria. Sergius of Resaina (d. 536) made a translation. Another was done by Phocas (seventh and beginning of eighth centuries), with notes from John of Scythopolis. John, Bishop of Dara, commented on the two *Hierarchies*.[3]

Dionysius greatly influenced Isaac of Nineveh, whose master remains, however, Evagrius. Simon of Taibutheh (d. 680) cites Dionysius. He refers to "no-knowledge or rather to a knowledge that is higher, than all knowledge." He also refers to Dionysius regarding angels and deification.

John Damescene (675–749) follows Dionysius in his teachings on God and on angels. There are also influences on the thought of Moses Bar Kepha, Denis Bar Salibi and Bar Hebraeus.

## The Dionysian Universe

The world of Dionysius can best be described as a circular movement of good, from the Good and toward the Good. In this hierarchical structure all is ordered and is accomplished in order, an order which is at once an arrangement *(taxis, cosmos)* and a commandment from God.

Dionysius himself speaks of the process as an "illumination" which proceeds by degrees and weakens as it moves further and further from its source, thereby bringing about a hierarchy. The hierarchy is therefore a hierarchy of illumination.

Dionysius conceives of the hierarchy not as a static and immobile order but as a movement of knowledge and of life which "descends from the Father of Lights" and reveals the going out and effusion of this Light so as to lead us back finally to the "deifying simplicity of the Father who gathers" through Jesus Christ, "light of the Father."

The human soul in its turn, from the illumination received from the scriptures (the very holy *Logia*, "the ray of the holy thearchic words") and from the gift of primordial light, is raised toward the simple ray of the Light itself.

The goal of hierarchy is

> to enable beings to be as like as possible to God and to be at one with him . . . Hierarchy causes its members to be images of God in all respects, to be clear and spotless mirrors reflecting the glow of . . . God himself. It ensures that when its members have received this full and divine splendor they can then pass on this light generously . . . to beings further down the scale.[4]

To be a member of a "hierarchy," as Dionysius understands it, is both to occupy a certain place on the universal scale of beings and to exercise a certain function. A being has its very nature defined by its degree of distance from God. Pure intelligences are at the top, matter is at the bottom. Moreover, each and every member of this universal hierarchy receives divine illumination which makes it to be, and to be what it is, only in order to transmit it, in turn, to a lower rank. Illumination is referred to more explicitly than knowledge in the descending process; knowledge is stressed more in the anagogic or ascending movement of the intellects.

There are three hierarchies: thearchic, angelic and human. Each hierarchy includes triads, subdivided into orders. Every hierarchy including the angelic is constituted by three elements: order (purification), knowledge (illumination) and activity. The role of every hierarchy is divinization. Divinization can be obtained by knowledge of divine things *(episteme)* or by holy activity *(energeia)*. It is by a constant effort of purification and conversion that we are assimilated and unified with God and thereby divinized.

At the highest level, bearing the title of Thearchy, is the Word, who is a unique principle and the cause and perfection of all hierarchy. The Word Incarnate is initiator of our intelligence. He effects the descending movement which illuminates all orders and the anagogic movement which perfects and gathers them.

The divine light and the being which it confers are an illuminative cascade whose steps are described by the treatises *On Celestial Hierarchy* and *On Ecclesiastical Hierarchy*. This "illumination" must be conceived not as a simple gift of light to already existing beings but as the gift of light which *is* their very being. What we call creation, then, is the very revelation or manifestation of God through his works. Dionysius calls this manifestation a "theophany."[5]

There is a bond among the various beings, but it is the divine goodness and divine peace which assure universal accord. The intelligences commune in friendship. Divine wisdom achieves this harmony and brings about a common effort and communion. However, the Dionysian universe is a hierarchical universe in which the differences of the diverse ranks are never abolished; the intelligences participate unequally in the gifts of divine illumination.

The circular movement which comes from God to constitute and transfigure the intellects returns in love from the intellects to God and continues anew to infinity. One's intellect progressively reaches its true dimensions in ascending from imperfect *analogia* and *symmetria* to the *analogia* and *symmetria* which have for their object divine ideas and wishes. Although characterized by order, the Dionysian universe is achieved and unified through liberty.

As we shall see below, while God is unknowable in himself, we have some intimation of him through the divine names that come down to us through hierarchy. Therefore, divinization is partly achieved through approaching God "through the hierarchy, in the midst of which the 'divine names' will be elaborated and purified."[6] Among the divine names, love plays a particularly important part because it is through divine love that all beings that radiate from God strive to return to him as to their source. Love is in each being as an active energy which draws each being out of itself in order to bring it back to God. This is what we mean when we say that of its very nature, love is "ecstatic" *(exstare)*. Its natural effect is to place the lover outside of himself and to transform him into the object of his love. From this point of view, the universal circulation of being, from the Good and toward the Good, is a circulation of divine love. Its effect in this life, and its term in the future life, is a certain divinization *(theosis)* of the loving creature whose love assimilates it to, and unites it with, God.[7]

Regarding the angelic hierarchies, only the first triad has direct relations with the Thearchy. The two others are related to God through the first triad.

The human or ecclesiastical hierarchy is situated between the celestial hierarchy and the legal hierarchy of the Old Testament. The ecclesiastical hierarchy is intermediate in that it shares qualities of the other two: with the angelic it partakes of intellectual contemplations; with the hierarchy of the Old Testament (whose understanding was tied to tangible things) it must rely on a variety of sensible symbols by which it is raised toward the divine.

There are two triads in this ecclesiastical hierarchy, the initiating and the initiated. The initiating consists of bishops, priests and ministers. The initiated is composed of monks, holy people and those to be purified.

The head of the hierarchy, the bishop, communicates not directly with God but through the heavenly hierarchy. However, within the hierarchy the bishop occupies the order of union *(enosis)*, of knowledge *(gnosis, episteme)* and of perfection, the priests have the task of illumination, and the deacons and the lesser orders the purifying function. The bishop confers directly all the sacred orders, baptizes catechumens and consecrates monks.

Monks achieve Christian philosophy, which consists not of the wisdom of the foolish but of knowing God by living in him and conforming to him. This manner of life brings about illumination and knowledge.

Beneath the monks, who form the order of perfection, the holy people constitute the order of contemplators or illumined, which is cared for by the middle order of the sacerdotal hierarchy.

The orders of those "to be purified" (catechumens, possessed, penitents) are entrusted to the lesser ministers, who "sanctify them in order that, perfectly purified, they are able to accede to the illuminating contemplation and to the communion of the sacraments the most rich of light." Not yet initiated into the sacraments or provisionally excluded from their communion, these orders are considered as profane orders. All the actions of the ministers toward orders of the "to be purified" are to aid them to fulfill the conditions of purification.

In the Dionysian context, all orders are taught from on high and taught by others. Two sources that nourish the earthly hierarchy are scripture and tradition. The scriptures are the thearchic, divine oracles transmitted to us by divine tradition and imposed on us as a divine law or ordinance, as a rule of thought and conduct.

Humans can receive illumination only under material conditions. From the symbols the soul is raised up *(anagetai)* to contemplation. *Anagogé* (elevation) consists of a type of abandon, a dynamic process by which God raises us by the means he has chosen for us to commune with him.[8]

### Sacred Scripture

Scripture is life and the door of life. This notion of scripture leaves no place for profane wisdom. Dionysius affirms that nothing can be said about God that is not found in, or cannot be proven by, holy scripture. God alone knows himself; he alone, then, can make himself known to those who seek him with humility. Even in scripture God speaks of himself in terms borrowed from creatures that represent him in various ways; but the names given to God in scripture require some interpretation.

The symbols of sacred scripture constitute the first field on which Dionysian contemplation is exercised. Biblical symbolism is a condescension to the intellect engaged in the world of matter. We ought to rise from material figures to the intelligible and holy realities that these figures represent. Anagogic *theoria* involves always purifying the image of materiality. In his work *The Divine Names,* Dionysius tells us that by the power of the Spirit "we reach a union superior to anything available to us by way of our own abilities or activities in the realm of the intellect." Therefore, we should not dare to use our own concepts regarding the "hidden divinity."[9]

We cannot know God directly and therefore we cannot name him directly. The only way correctly to name him from the names of creatures involves a threefold operation. First, we affirm that God is what scripture says he is: One, Lord, Powerful, Just and so forth. Vladimir Lossky describes this process (cataphatic theology) as a ladder by which the soul can mount to contemplation. The names of God revealed in scripture are not ideas or concepts formed by our intellects but are rather images or ideas intended to guide our minds to a contemplation "which transcends all understanding."[10]

Second, theologians know that such notions as oneness, lordship and power cannot possibly apply to God in the same sense as to creatures; hence, for them, the necessity of denying that God is any one of those things in the only sense which we can give to their names.

Affirmative and negative theology are reconciled in a third operation, which consists in saying that God deserves these names in a sense that is inconceivable to human reason, because it is incomparably higher than that which applies to creatures. This Dionysius calls "superlative theology." He has given a striking example of his method in his short treatise, *The Mystical Theology.* The conclusion of this work is a series of negations followed by a series of negations of these negations, for God is above all negations and all affirmations. What is affirmed about God is beneath him. His not being light does not mean that he is darkness; his not being truth does not mean that he is error; rather, because God is the inaccessible Cause of all things, he transcends both what can be affirmed and what can be denied of him from our knowledge of his effects.

## The Sacraments

The goal of the life of the Church and its teaching is divinization. The Dionysian definition of sacrament is essentially conceived as a triple activity of purification, illumination and perfection.

The life of divinized intellects has its origin and source in the "sacrament of illumination" (baptism); it is developed and completed in the other sacraments: sacraments of "union" (the eucharist), of holy oil, of sacerdotal ordination, of monastic consecration and of funerals.

Besides the contemplation arising from the study of scripture and natural symbols, the sacramental liturgy also engages our spiritual faculties. Very often in *The Ecclesiastical Hierarchy, theoria* designates the spiritual ("anagogic") study which is made regarding each of the sacramental rites or the meaning of each of the sacraments.

Baptism is the sacrament of divine birth or of illumination. In conferring on us a divine existence, it permits us to act divinely. It is necessary if we are to pass from the profane world, which is that of evil and shadows, to the luminous universe of the hierarchy. The rite of baptism is the seal of this participation in the light, which divinizes the person and allows him to commune in the divine heritage. Baptism renders possible sacramental *theoria:* it constitutes a contemplating order. Catechumens are brought into the "theoretical" order *(theoretiké taxis)* by the instruction they receive from the deacons and by the illumination conferred by the sacrament of baptism. On the other hand, the non-baptized, the penitents and the possessed are the orders to be purified.[11]

The essential characteristic of the eucharist is that it unites. It confers upon us a communion and union to the One. The final initiation into the eucharist, reserved to the supreme hierarch (bishop), allows those who have received it the perfection to participate in the perfective knowledge of the holy mysteries; and the eucharist provides the highest possibility of contemplation.[12]

## Theoria

The progressive freeing from images and schemas (figures) permits the intellect to approach contemplation and the knowledge of the intelligible names of God. In *theoria* one ought to avoid articulating God with concepts any more than with schemas and images, for anthropomorphisms of the intellect are just as dangerous as those of the senses. There are various degrees of *theoria:* sensible representations, liturgical and sacramental contemplation and intelligible contemplation of the names of God. Negative theology corrects our thoughts and reaches up to the threshold of ecstasy. *Theoria* is essentially anagogic; the mind must progressively abandon all orders of created reality, which have enabled its ascension.

The functions of *theoria* are on the one hand negative and cathartic, purging away the inadequacies of the symbols from which it arises, and on the other hand positive and anagogical, leading up to union with God. As we have noted, there is a contemplation of the diverse images in which divine truth is communicated in scripture as well as contemplation of the symbolic rites of the liturgy.[13]

One arrives at purified *theoria* by the abandonment of the sensible and the intelligible that one surpasses in a new mode of knowledge. In *The Mystical Theology*, it seems that *theoria* as such does not attain to God himself: Moses contemplated the place where God is and not God himself. The ultimate goal of *theoria* appears, then, to be the experiential knowledge, transcending all symbolism and all discourse, that God is unknowable. In this union, therefore, the intellect is more passive than active.[14]

This knowledge is of a new type, since it is not borrowed from any sensible elements or discursive stages of thought. For this reason Dionysius defines it in negative terms such as "unknowing," indicating God's transcendence.

## Mystical Ignorance (Unknowing)

Dionysius rejects Origen's teaching that one could achieve knowledge of God's essence. Humans know only "beings." God is above being and superior to all opposition between being and non-being. Ultimate union with God is by way of "ignorance" rather than through knowledge. Therefore, this achievement is beyond the senses or the intellect. God is manifest by his "powers" rather than by his essence. The God of Dionysius is not the "One" (the transcendent principle) of Plotinus but the living God of the Bible.

To know God as above all affirmation and all negation, that is, to know that he cannot be known, is the mystical ignorance that constitutes the supreme degree of knowledge. In contemplating God, one must realize that what he is really contemplating is not God but one of his creatures. Ignorance is necessarily the highest form of knowledge, where knowledge strives to attain an object that lies beyond being.

One must renounce sense and all the workings of reason and achieve perfect ignorance. When one goes beyond what is known, the "mysteries of theology, simple, unconditional, invariable are laid bare in a darkness of silence beyond the light." The darkness of the mystical experience contains a knowledge higher than the "fundamental reasons" of theology. The distinction between subject and object fades. Action and passion are blurred. To arrive at this union with him who transcends all being and all knowledge, one must undergo purification ("catharsis"). One leaves behind all heavenly sounds and words and reaches the silence of unknowing in which the cause of all things dwells beyond all affirmation and negation. Thus one can penetrate the darkness where he who is beyond all created things makes his dwelling.

Describing the vision of Moses, Dionysius says that the prophet was then freed from the objects and the organs even of contemplation, and penetrated the mystical "cloud of unknowing," wherein he closed his eyes to all apprehension of knowledge and became situated in the intangible and the absolute invisible. Moses is united to the absolutely Unknowable by the cessation of all knowledge and, in this total unknowing, he knows a knowing that surpasses intelligence.[15]

The "catharsis" that is called for is not just purifying the intellect from the multiplicity of created things of Neo–Platonism but rather involves going beyond being as it conceals divine non-being, renouncing the created to gain access to the uncreated. Essentially conceived as rupture and negativity, ecstasy imposes on the intelligence an abandonment and radical renouncing that makes one reject not only the products of intellectual activity but the intellectual activity itself. Ecstasy is the ultimate act of intellectual renunciation, the summit of love that dispossesses itself. In Platonism, the goal was union with the "One," a primordial and ontological union with God. In Dionysius, there is a series of changes, transitions from the created to the uncreated, resulting in the acquisition of something that one did not possess.[16]

In *The Divine Names* Dionysius explains, as we have seen, why God reveals himself in names such as Good, Life, Wisdom and Power; but he explains also that a more elevated understanding of God, "the most divine knowledge of God," is that which one obtains by ignorance, in virtue of the intellect going out of itself and being united to the more luminous rays that shine forth from on high in the unsoundable depth of Wisdom. Dionysius calls this knowledge "mystical theology"; it is established in the soul emptied of all representation of the natural order.[17] Dionysius therefore substitutes for the intellectualism and the *gnosis* of the Origenists apophatism and ecstasy.

Dionysius does not have the same confidence as Evagrius in the "proper activity of the intellect" or even in the marvelous efficaciousness of the commandments in leading the intellect to the Holy Trinity. He relies much more on passivity than activity: purification done by superior hierarchies and submitted to by inferior ones. At the summit is ecstasy *(theia pathon)*, the violence of desire tearing one away from the intellect enclosed in its proper laws, in order to be thrown into the divine darkness. Evagrius is ignorant of ecstasy in the proper sense of the word, and Origin rejects it.[18]

## Contemplation and Ecstasy

Contemplation is found to be not an end in itself but a means toward an ecstatic moment of love that goes beyond knowledge. Not only is love the motive force behind the intellectual processes, but in its ultimate stage of *ecstasis* love is the activity into which contemplation leads. Contemplation gives way to the ecstatic abandonment of self in which deification occurs.

It is difficult to fix a line between *theoria* on the one side and ecstasy and darkness on the other. *Theoria* finds its normal achievement in ecstasy, which surpasses it without annihilating it. Darkness represents the place and modality of mystical apprehension, superior to the opposition of subject knowing and object known.

There is a difference between negative theology and mystical contemplation. The former remains a discursive limit of the intellect, while contemplation is situated beyond discursiveness. Negative theology limits and corrects the formulations of affirmative theology. Mystic contemplation refers to none of these steps; it is a pure, immaterial vision from which sense and intelligence are radically excluded. Ecstasy presupposes a total detachment of all things and of self. Ecstasy is above all union with God *(enosis)* and divinization *(theosis)*. The intellect is united with superluminous rays.[19]

It is the absolute transcendence of God that necessitates the doctrine of darkness. But while divine transcendence is constantly affirmed in the works of Dionysius, they habitually present God as intelligible light, superior to all light and the source from whom flows all light. This affirmation establishes a doctrine of illumination while the transcendence of God is safeguarded; for the source and principle of all light is beyond all light. The symbol of darkness expresses this transcendence.[20]

In *The Divine Names* Dionysius declares,

> But when our souls are moved by intelligent energies in the direction of the things of the intellect then our senses and all that go with them are no longer needed. And the same happens with our intelligent powers which, when the soul becomes divinized, concentrate sightlessly and through an unknowing union on the rays of "unapproachable light."[21]

The true light remains hidden to those who possess it. The divine darkness is this inaccessible light "where it is said that God dwells." The mysteries of "theology are discovered in the darkness more than luminous in the silence which reveals secrets" (*Mystical Theology* I, 1, 997ab, etc.). There is therefore an unknowing or a mystique of darkness that surpasses light itself.[22]

An objection can be raised that if for Dionysius all union with God works through the mediation of the hierarchies, how is direct ecstasy between humans and God possible? A possible answer might lie in the doctrine that the Word Incarnate is the head of all hierarchies and we have been given the ability to be united with Christ.[23]

## Conclusion

With Dionysius we have a clear articulation of the mysteriousness of God on the one hand and God's revealing of himself on the other. He integrates this theological worldview with a developed theory of contemplation, which begins with meditating on the earthly symbols and images of God and culminates in ignorance and unknowing. The stage of darkness expresses a God who is absolutely inaccessible, invisible, intangible, unnameable, escaping all grasp and all determination.

As mentioned before, Dionysius, in sharp contrast to Origen and Evagrius, sees the goal of contemplation to be not knowledge of God but an ignorance that crosses the threshold of the presence of God in mystery. Nevertheless, God is Light and his rays go forth in creation to illumine and reveal. For Dionysius, the sacraments themselves, besides bringing about sanctification, are vehicles of illumination and sources of contemplation. By meditating on the scriptures, the Divine Names and the sacraments, we are able to climb anagogically to the source of light. The energizing force is ultimately that of love.

Union with the holy is the fruit of love and the consummation of desire, the point at which one enters into possession and enjoyment. Union takes place in the unknowing darkness that is superior to light. As with Moses, it is a cloud of unknowing in which by knowing nothing, he knew beyond understanding. The cloud is dark because of the excess of light. On entering the cloud we pass from the ordinary negations of apophatic theology to a complete cessation of word and understanding.[24]

In this mystical union with God, however, his nature remains incomprehensible. Making affirmations and denials about attributes borrowed from created things says nothing about the Cause, who is above all denial.

In *The Divine Names* Dionysius notes, "The most divine knowledge of God, that which comes through unknowing, is achieved in a union far beyond mind, when mind turns away from all things, even from itself, and when it is made one with the dazzling rays, being then and there enlightened by the inscrutable depth of Wisdom."[25] In union, man belongs wholly to the Unknowable and is therefore deified.

# 7
# Martyrius *(Sahdona)*

Martyrius (a Greek translation of the Syriac name *Sahdona*) represents for us a writer in the Syriac tradition who writes about the ascetical life from years of experience as a monk and as a solitary. While pure prayer and contemplation are the ultimate goal of the spiritual life, Martyrius devotes his attention to the long process of asceticism that is required before one can progress to perfection. Martyrius is completely imbued with the sacred scriptures; his writings are remarkable for the hundreds of biblical passages he integrates into every chapter of his teaching.

Martyrius was born toward the end of the sixth century in the village Halmon in the region of Beit Nuhadré (which is in the vicinity of Kirkus in modern Iraq.) Due to the influence of his mother and the example of a holy woman, Shirin, a close friend of his mother, he entered the monastery of Beit Abé at an early age around 615–620. Between 635–40, he became bishop of Beit Garmai (the region around Kirkus.) He was involved in Christological controversy and accused of anti-Nestorian teaching. Deposed by a synod, he was sent into exile. He was recalled due to the intervention of influential friends but refused to retract and was sent back into exile. He ended his days as a solitary living near Edessa.

Martyrius's works dealing with the Christological controversies have been lost. The writings that survive concern the ascetical life. His major work, which has become a classic of monastic writing in the Syriac tradition, is the *Book of Perfection*, which has survived almost intact. It is more a work of spiritual counseling than one of systematic theology. There are also five letters to his fellow monks and a book of maxims of wisdom. As already noted, Martyrius cites the Bible with great frequency. In the edition of his writings prepared by A. de Halleux, of the 499 pages of text there are 5,337 citations or allusions from the Bible: 1,589 from the Old Testament, especially the Psalms, Isaiah, Genesis, Sirach and Exodus; and 3,748 from the New Testament.[1]

Martyrius appears to have depended especially on Ephrem, Basil of Caesarea and Gregory of Nazianzus. He also cites John Chrysostom and probably felt the influence of others, especially Theodore of Mopsuestia.[2]

## The Book of Perfection

The *Book of Perfection* is divided into two parts. In the first part, which contains treatises and chapters, the first treatise and most of the second are lost. In the chapters that survive, Martyrius invites the reader to choose the narrow road involving separation from the world, austerity, the battle against the passions, poverty and bearing injuries. The goal of asceticism is a positive one, namely, to become disposed to possess invisible realities. By means of the assiduous contemplation of God and heavenly things, we are able to lose sight of earthly things.[3]

The third treatise praises the solitary life and presents John the Baptist as its model. One must follow the rule of abnegation, becoming a stranger to the world. The most powerful weapon against Satan is humility, and the monk should become "as one intoxicated with the charity of Christ" and seized by the drunkenness of the love of God, as were St. Paul, the apostles and the martyrs. The monk should love tranquility, peace and serenity and seek to converse with God in assiduous prayer at every moment.[4]

The fourth treatise is consecrated to the fear of the Lord. Martyrius teaches that God chooses not to do all the work of the spiritual life alone and that we must show some effort. However, in reality, God's grace is necessary for every step of the spiritual life. On the other hand, the monk must not believe that he can progress in the spiritual life casually. God demands that we show serious effort so that we may experience the fruits of our endeavors, although in reality all depends on God.

Martyrius also speaks of the relationship of the cenobitic (monastic) to the solitary life. The solitary life is compared to that of the angels standing before God in recollection of spirit. However, the achieving of this goal involves violent and terrifying struggles. Therefore, the cenobitic life is a necessary first stage. He advises that it is necessary to accept the "yoke of fraternal submission" and the "arduous training of life in common." If one regresses, he should return to the community. Martyrius notes that very few have lived the solitary life. Even the Desert Fathers were accompanied by one or more companions. Although the solitary life is the way of perfection, the cenobitic life is advised for the majority.[5]

THEOLOGICAL VIRTUES

The second part of the *Book of Perfection*, which consists of fourteen chapters, is developed in a more orderly fashion. Besides an introductory and a concluding chapter, three chapters are devoted to the theological virtues and the nine remaining to the following themes: abnegation, continence, fasting, prayer, penance, humility, obedience, constancy and vigilance.

The theological virtues are the foundation not only of the Christian life but of the monastic life. Martyrius calls for purity of heart and for love. The person who possesses love becomes the abode of the Trinity. The author declares,

> Happy is that person of love who has caused God, who is love, to dwell in his heart.
> Happy are you, O heart, so small and confined, yet you have caused him whom heaven and earth cannot contain to dwell spiritually in your womb, as in a restful abode.
> Happy that luminous eye of the heart which, in its purity, clearly beholds him before whose sight the seraphs veil their face. . . .
> Happy are you, mortal body made out of dust, wherein resides the Fire that sets the worlds alight. . . .
> It is truly a matter for wonder and astonishment that he, before whom the heavens are not pure, who puts awe into his angels, should take delight and pleasure in a heart of flesh that is filled with love for him, that is open to him, that is purified so as to act as his holy dwelling place, joyfully serving and ministering to him in whose presence thousand upon thousand, ten thousand upon ten thousand fiery angels stand in awe, as they minister to his glory.[6]

Martyrius teaches that vowed celibacy should be expressed in love of God and in diligence in doing good. The purpose of renouncing the world is to prepare oneself for the goal of the spiritual life, namely, the heavenly city. One seeks to become a citizen of another world. Self-abnegation is the basis for continence or chastity and is supported by fasting. Abstinence sketches on the mortal body an image of immortal life and reveals the condition of the new age.[7]

PRAYER

Chapter eight is devoted to prayer. Prayer must be rooted in humility. It is a matter of the heart and becomes unacceptable if our heart is not purified of passions or if we pray without respect.

Prayer demands that we be attentive, that we collect our thoughts and set a careful watch on the intellect. Our spiritual ministry before God should be accompanied with "a sense of awe and trembling with the spiritual fervor of joy and deep love."[8]

With our mind and thoughts recollected, we can be lifted above earth and become like those who stand in heaven. We can converse with God, "stretching out towards him the gaze of the eyes of our heart; in a hidden way [we] look upon his majesty in awe, and behold as though in a mirror as it were the likeness of Him who cannot be seen."[9]

If our prayer is without blemish, God will accept it and be pleased with our offering. Looking upon the purity of our heart, God through the Spirit will raise us towards heaven. Martyrius declares,

> Then we shall behold the Lord, to our delight and not to our destruction, as the stillness of his revelation falls upon us and the hidden things of the knowledge of him will be portrayed in us; our hearts will be given spiritual joy, along with hidden mysteries which I am unable to disclose in words to the simple.[10]

Those standing in Christ's presence are engaged in divine realities and are freed from this world. They are called to persevere in the "hidden prayer of the heart" and reject all worldly concerns. As noted above, the cares of this world can be an obstacle to pure prayer. Also reiterated is the fact that the help of the Holy Spirit is needed in our ascent but that we must do our part in purifying our mind.

By continually directing our thoughts to God, we will purify our soul. The reading of the sacred scriptures improves the quality of our prayer. Martyrius claims that the "divine words polish away rust from the mind and lighten it of the weight of earthly things." Meditation on the scriptures engenders love and purity.

It is praiseworthy to spend the whole night before the Sunday celebration in prayer and the chanting of psalms. Ideally we should pray constantly and not limit ourselves to the recitation of the Office at fixed times.

When we admit our guilt and repent of our sins, God in his mercy will draw close and sanctify us in his love. With the fire of his Spirit, he burns away our impurities; he illuminates our darkness with the light of his revelation. We are thus called to undistracted service and prayer before his presence in awe and love.[11] Ultimately, repentance is gained through active love.

### MONASTIC VIRTUES

Martyrius gives high importance to humility. Humility can erase our sins and completely remove their stain. In one of his letters to monks, Martyrius responds to a monk who sought to transfer to another monastery where he could be more re-collected. He advises that recollection is not a matter of place but of the heart, and that recollection is achieved through humility and scorning of oneself.[12]

In discussing obedience, Martyrius stresses that it should be mutual and universal. All should care for one another and serve one another. Those who are charged with a public office should serve their brothers "with simplicity of heart, humbly and in all purity, as if they were our Lord."[13]

Martyrius concludes his study of the monastic virtues with a chapter on vigilance. We must be watchful in actions, words and thoughts. This vigilance is especially required when we stand before God in the spiritual ministry of prayer. "At such a time it is appropriate that we stand with a wakeful and attentive mind, combining a sense of awe and trembling with the spiritual fervor of joy and deep love."[14]

Vigilance is maintained through spiritual reading, meditation on the word of God, prayer of the heart and contemplation. One should not judge others, but rather try to find the good in every person, no matter what a sinner he or she might be.[15]

In his fifth letter to monks, Martyrius provides further observations on the solitary life and perfect contemplation. He teaches that the "ineffable mystery of unity," already prefigured in baptism, "is accomplished especially and in the most superior fashion with the perfect." Although they still contemplate the enigma in its reflections, they are transformed by degrees and rise from unity to unity towards it.[16]

A principal theme in Martyrius's writings is the necessity of limpidity of intention and transparence of heart. He cites especially two scriptural passages as the basis of this teaching, namely, Matthew 5:8: "Blessed are the pure of heart, for they shall see God," and Matthew 6:22: "If your eye is sound, your entire body will be filled with light." Martyrius observes that just as our eye never tires of new sights, so if the illumined eye of the mind is pure, it is able to glimpse the mysteries of divine knowledge. The more purified it becomes, the closer it can approach the "essential light of the divinity":

> When the vision of the body's eye is clear and its light is mingled with the luminous rays of the sun, it is able to see the sun's light. Analogously, when the heart is purified and the eye of awareness is illumined, the light of its vision being commingled with the essential radiance of the Spirit of God, then, by means of the radiance of the grace from the spiritual brightness provided from above, the heart begins to behold, in a spiritual way, the great Sun of Righteousness and to enjoy his beauty.[17]

If the monk is devoted to purity of heart and contemplation, the Holy Spirit will dwell in him and be experienced by him. The Spirit nourishes the soul, which then constantly praises God. Martyrius even refers to the soul as a "hidden church" giving worship. He challenges the soul to a continual praise and recollection of God's name. "Let us sculpt out the beauty of our souls by gazing on the likeness of his glory, so that we may be seen to be glorious statues of his divinity within creation."[18]

Martyrius goes on to explain that when God created us, he clothed us in his image and likeness and adorned us with the glory of his divinity, "making us as secondary gods on earth." Our response should be to offer worship and glory, since God has mingled our spirit with his Spirit and imbued us with his grace, so that the fire of the Holy Spirit bursts forth in us.[19]

However, as noted above, while our efforts are essential to progress in the spiritual life, nothing can be achieved without the grace of God. At the end of the *Book of Perfection*, Martyrius admits that even when reaching the door of heaven, by his own ability he does not know how to enter or to adore or pray. Only through the Holy Spirit can he approach with assurance, adore in truth and confess the divine name.

# 8

# Isaac of Nineveh

Isaac of Nineveh witnesses for us a later stage of Syriac spirituality. By this time, the major lines of various spiritual world views and methodologies had been practiced and reworked in many areas of the Christian East. Isaac himself represents the Syriac tradition as it was lived in the Nestorian church and especially in the region of the Persian Gulf. His spiritual teachings manifest maturity and a deep understanding of the contemplative life. His writings were translated into Arabic and Greek and had widespread influence which extended to the Byzantine world.

Isaac of Nineveh lived in the second half of the seventh century. He was a native of Qatar on the Persian Gulf and was consecrated Bishop of Nineveh by the Catholicos George. He did not have administrative ability and therefore resigned the episcopal see after five months and joined the hermits in the mountain of Matout in the country of Beth Huzayé. We are told that he left the anchoritic life to enter the Monastery of Rabban Shabur, where he applied himself to the study of the scriptures so intensely that he went blind because of his reading and austerity. Having become blind, he dictated his works to his disciples. He died at an advanced age and was buried in the Monastery of Rabban Shabur.[1]

Sebastian Brock informs us that Isaac is not a systematic writer and that his spirituality draws on many different sources: Evagrius, John of Apamea (whose threefold pattern of spiritual life he sometimes employs), the Macarian Homilies, the Apophthegmata and related literature of the Egyptian Fathers, Theodore of Mopsuestia (to whom Isaac normally refers as "the Exegete"), Abba Isaiah and Mark the Hermit. Although Dionysius the Areopagite (whose works had been translated into Syriac in the early sixth century) is also mentioned by Isaac on a few occasions, he does not appear to have had a formative influence on Isaac's thought.[2]

The spiritual doctrine of Isaac, like that of all mystics, has as its goal to lead the monk to the contemplation of God in a mode of life which already anticipates celestial life. But the road there is

long and arduous because of the obstacles that must be conquered, the suggestions of the demon that must be discerned and
combated, the attachments and memories of the soul which have
damaged its true nature. Finally, there is the inaccessibility of
God, who is given only in grace and remains out of reach. Even
those who have traveled the whole road of asceticism must live in
hope and wait until he reveals himself.[3]

As mentioned above, Isaac was influenced by Evagrius of Pontus. His system rests on the distinction between body, soul and
spirit. To each of these parts of the person there is a distinct
operation. Therefore, the spiritual life involves three levels:
praxis, natural contemplation, and contemplation of God, or theology. The three operations are the corporeal, the psychic (relating
to the lower operations of the soul) and the spiritual, which must
be accomplished to reach contemplation.

## The Corporeal Step

The monk ought first to combat his passions whose seat is the
body, so the first step is called the corporeal step or corporeal
conduct. On this level one is called to perform those corporeal
works which will purify the body by the exercise of virtue in
exterior works. Life in solitude is the indispensable condition for
this step that Isaac calls "corporeal conduct in solitude." For Isaac,
one is able to approach God only if one is removed from the
world. Passions are not eliminated nor evil thoughts dissipated
outside of the desert. Without solitude, man is not able to penetrate into himself to recognize his passions and to combat them.[4]

To despoil oneself of all things is equally necessary if one is to
succeed in the battle against the passions. To conquer the world
signifies conquering all cravings for it. Passions are the elements
that control the movement of the world; when the passions cease,
the world stops in its movement. These passions ought to be
combated by exterior or "corporeal" practices. Isaac recommends
before all things fasting, with vigil and psalmody in the service of
the Lord, crucifying the body all night against the pleasure of
sleep, as the beginning of the holy way toward God and the
foundation of all virtues.

For Isaac, withdrawal from and renunciation of the world
means not the physical removal of oneself to a monastery or the
desert but separation from "bodily behavior and carnal thoughts";

dealing with the "world" involves our interior state. Renunciation of this inner world of self is essential for anyone who wants to draw near to God; it involves a radical re-orientation of one's life and attitudes. Isaac offers a simple test by which one can discover to what extent one is living in the world. If, upon self-examination, you find yourself moved by "love of riches, the accumulation of belongings, self-indulgence (which gives rise to sexual desire), love of honor (which is the source of envy), the exercise of authority, self-esteem and pride of office, self-enhancement, a high reputation among men (which gives rise to resentment), or fear for one's body," then you are indeed still in the world—even though you may be living physically in a secluded cell.[5]

The first virtue of the corporeal step is the fear of the Lord, which is engendered in the heart following the renouncing of the world and fortified by the meditation on future judgment. "Repentance is a grace. It is a second birth of God. We receive the pledge of it in baptism." This corporeal step is characterized by recognition that the monk ought to impose on himself the practice of exterior virtues because he is still incapable of meditating on his interior self. The practice of constraint is an indispensable virtue to one who is on the road toward God. "Perseverance in trials is the crucifixion of the body."[6]

## HUMILITY

The crucifixion of the self is by no means confined to ascetic practices; it also involves "compelling ourselves perpetually to be inwardly full of mercy towards all kinds of rational beings at all times."

> If, on the other hand, out of compassion, you seek to turn him [one with whom you are angry] to the truth, then you will actually suffer on his behalf. You will speak just a word or two to him in tears and love; you will not flare up at him, but you will banish from your countenance any sign of hostility. Love does not know how to get angry or indignant, it does not reprimand in a hurtful way. The sign of the presence of real love and knowledge is a profound humility issuing from the inner mind.[7]

"Humility," Isaac points out, "is the very garment of the Divinity, for the Word who became man clothed himself in it." Whoever would imitate Christ, then, must likewise "wrap himself" in humility. In his *Discourse VIII* Isaac tells us,

Humility restrains the heart. Then, once someone has become humble, immediately God's mercy surrounds him and embraces him. Once this mercy has drawn close, the heart straightaway becomes aware of its benefit, for a certain confidence and power surge up within it. Having become aware of the advent of divine succor to support and help it, then the heart is immediately filled with faith.[8]

A hint of what this humility implies is given in a famous passage which describes the threefold end towards which the Christian should strive: repentance, purity and perfection:

What is repentance? "The desisting from former sins and suffering on account of them." What sums up purity? "A heart that feels compassion for every created being." And what is perfection? "Profound humility, which consists in the abandonment of everything visible and invisible." Now the visible comprises everything to do with the senses, and the invisible means all thoughts on such subjects . . .

On another occasion the same Old Man was asked, What is humility? "The embracing of a voluntary mortification with respect to everything." And what is a compassionate heart? "The heart that is inflamed in this way embraces the entire creation—man, birds, animals, and even demons." At the recollection of them, and at the sight of them, such a man's eyes fill with tears that arise from the great compassion which presses on his heart. The heart grows tender and cannot endure to hear of or look upon any injury or even the smallest suffering inflicted upon anything in creation. For this reason such a man prays increasingly with tears even for irrational animals and for the enemies of truth and for all who harm it, that they may be guarded and be forgiven. The compassion, which pours out from his heart without measure, like God's, extends even to reptiles.[9]

As long as a person is still on this corporeal step, he is incapable of true prayer, which supposes an elevation above terrestrial things. Isaac advises one to persevere in corporeal practice without pretending to be elevated to the degree of contemplative prayer.

## The Psychic Step

The principal task of the psychic step is the purification of the soul by means of the battle against thoughts strange to its nature, thus reestablishing the soul in its primordial nature, where it is pure and exempt from all passion. "By its nature the soul is not subject to passion . . . We believe that God has not created His image subject to suffering. His image say I is not the body, but the soul which is invisible." The soul becomes passible following its union with the body. Isaac considers this doctrine on the nature of the soul as the official doctrine of the Church: "When the soul is moved in its passion, all the children of the Church confess that it has gone out of its nature. The passions have then entered into the nature of the soul."

We find this doctrine in another Syriac mystic, John the Solitary of Apamea, a century before: "The soul is superior to evil actions and to shameful thoughts, but because of the body, it is affected by its participation with them."

The purification of the soul takes place in two steps. It is necessary first to purify movements toward corruptible things in order to contemplate the wisdom that God has put in the soul. At this level of purification, the soul remains moved still by something exterior to its nature. At a higher degree of purification, the soul is turned completely from exterior things; no longer excited by exterior things, its movements spring forth from its very nature, which has returned to its original state. A person attains this state when he has guarded his senses and his memories in perfect solitude.[10]

Abandonment of the "world" is only one side of the coin; it must be accompanied by self-abandonment to divine care. This divine care "surrounds all men at all times, although it is seen only by those who have purified themselves from sins and who think of God perpetually: to such people it is revealed clearly." Self-abandonment upon God at the same time involves a perpetual consciousness of his presence:

> Sit before his face at all times, thinking of him and recollecting him in your heart. Otherwise, if you only come to see him after a long interval, you will not be able to speak freely with him because of your sense of shame. Freedom of speech is born from constancy; such constancy among men concerns only the things of the body, but with God it is the attitude of the soul, and the nearness brought about by prayer.[11]

Prayer is at the very center of Christian life. The aim of prayer is quite simply "to acquire love of God, for in prayer all the reasons for loving God are to be discovered." Elsewhere Isaac expresses the same idea in the form of an actual prayer:

Make me worthy to know you, my Lord, so that I may love you too. I do not desire the knowledge that involves distraction of the mind, that comes from the application of learning; rather, make me worthy of that knowledge whereby the mind comes to praise you as it gazes upon you with that gaze which banishes from the mind the sensations of the world. Make me worthy to be raised above the imaginings which my own will gives birth to, so that I am impelled to gaze upon the bonds of the cross with a continuous gaze such as nature does not give, thus crucifying my mind whose freedom has been rendered useless by its subjecting itself to impulse. Place in me the pure metal of your love, so that I may be removed from the world as I follow you; stir in me the awareness of that humility of yours wherein you lived in the world having put on the raiment of our body, so that, as I continuously recall it, I may accept with delight the humiliation of my own nature.[12]

The psychic step, therefore, is a labor of the heart which is performed without ceasing with meditation on the future judgment, in constant prayer of heart and in the consideration of God's providence and solicitude toward everything in the world. One must also guard against the interior passions lest they penetrate into the heart.

One can be mistaken about thoughts that arise in prayer. They can come from the right or the left. The thoughts of the right are able to be recognized by two sure signs, inflamed ardor of the heart and the pouring out of tears. The thoughts of the left, caused by the demon, provoke in the soul coldness and agitation. The "psychic" person passes thus through diverse states of warmth and coldness, of peace and agitation. These thoughts are presented sometimes under luminous appearances. The monk must give proof of a very sharp spirit of discernment aided by the reading of the scriptures: "The spiritual meditation of the intellect on the meaning of Scripture in view of the love of God closes the entries of the soul to strange thoughts and guards the understanding in the fervent reminder of future realities."

### THE GIFT OF TEARS

Isaac gives very great importance in his mystical doctrine to the gift of tears, which is the proper sign of the psychic state. In the measure that tears abound, the soul progresses on the road to attaining integrity or impassibility. For those who understand, tears are as the frontier between corporeality and spirituality, between the passionate state and purity.[13]

Having arrived at this point on its march toward God, the soul recovers integrity of its nature, that is, impassibility, the indispensable condition for contemplating God in his ineffable light. Impassibility is the summit of the corporeal and psychic steps. It consists of the complete immunity of the soul in regard to passions and exterior thoughts which still do not cease to assault it, but now without burning. Impassibility does not consist in not feeling passions; rather it is the refusal to submit to the passions.

The soul so purified becomes capable of pure prayer. It has become "an intellect empty of all thought of things below and a heart which has turned completely its regard to the desire of the future hope." Pure prayer is not possible before acquisition of immunity to all movements which come from outside. Pure prayer is aroused by the natural movements of the pure soul; "The movement of prayer is the effect of movements of the soul." For the purified soul, prayer becomes a constant state, which is the gift of the Holy Spirit.[14]

## The Spiritual Step

When the soul attains impassibility, in recovering its original integrity, it arrives at the threshold of the spiritual step, the summit of the mystical life which is beyond human possibility and is a purely gratuitous gift of God.[15] This illumined state constitutes a return to the "natural" state of the soul as it was originally created. Grace is able to bring out the soul's innate natural beauty just as spring brings out the beauty of the earth:

> The power of spring makes even the smallest plants in the valleys to bud, warming the earth as fire does a cauldron, so that it sends forth the treasures of the plants which God has laid in the earth's nature, to the joy of creation and to his glory. Likewise Grace makes manifest all the glory which God has hidden in the nature of the soul, showing the soul this glory and making it glad because of its own beauty.[16]

Human beings remain unworthy, even after having accomplished all the practices and overcome all the passions and strange thoughts. This door remains closed until it pleases God to open it. "The ascent to the cross consists of two parts: the crucifixion of the body, and the ascent to contemplation. The former is achieved by one's own free will, the latter by divine action."[17]

In his *Discourse XXII* Isaac observes,

And sometimes out of prayer contemplation *(theoria)* is born: this cuts prayer off from the lips, and the person who beholds this is like a corpse without soul in wonder. We call this the faculty of "vision in prayer"; it does not consist in any image or portrayable form, as foolish people say. This contemplation in prayer also has its degrees and different gifts, but up to this point it is still prayer, for thought has not yet passed into the state when there is non-prayer—for there is something even more excellent than prayer. For the movements of the tongue and of the heart during prayer act as the keys; what comes after these is the actual entry into the treasury: from this point onward mouth and tongue become still, as do the heart—the treasurer to the thoughts—the mind—governor of the senses—and the bold spirit—that swift bird—along with all the means and uses they possess. Requests too cease here, for the master of the house has come.[18]

When God permits humans to be elevated above the integrity of the soul to enter the region of spirituality, an abundant light suddenly floods the intellect, which is then directed by grace toward what is not given to the senses to know or understand. This light is faith, which at the highest degree of the mystical life substitutes for knowledge. "Knowledge is the ladder by which humans climb to the heights of faith and, when humans arrive there, there is no more need of knowledge." Faith here is the possibility "the soul has to contemplate the truth of God":

All the saints who were judged worthy of the spiritual conduct which is wonder *(tehro* in Syriac) in God, were led by the force of faith in the joy of this conduct superior to nature. I do not speak here of faith which consists in believing in the distinction of adorable Persons of the Divinity and in the properties of its nature and in the admirable economy *(mdabronuto* in Syriac) toward our humanity by the assumption of our nature; I speak rather of this faith which is the spiritual light which burns in the soul by grace.[19]

The loss of the use of the senses characterizes this state: "The spiritual life is practiced without the senses . . . The density of the body is then abolished and vision becomes spiritual." The intellect is found completely directed toward God "by the vision of his ineffable glory." Humans are henceforth liberated from all exterior practice and become exempt from laws and commandments: "All vigor of laws and commandments decreed by God to humans have their term in the purity of the heart."

This heavenly state does not seem to be a stable state in this life. It is a temporary surpassing of the normal human condition. Humans are ravished in ecstasy engendered by the love of God.

This ecstasy occurs by the intervention of the Holy Spirit during prayer, because the time of prayer is more propitious for the reception of so great a gift.[20] Isaac explains:

> All types and varieties of prayer which human beings address to God have their boundaries extending up to purity of heart. . . . Moving inwards from purity of prayer, once one has passed this boundary, the mind has no prayer, no movement, no tears, no authority, no freedom, no requests, no desire, no longing for anything that is hoped for in this world or the world to come. For this reason, after pure prayer there is no longer any prayer . . . But beyond the boundary, there exists wonder, not prayer. From that point onwards the mind ceases from prayer; there is the capacity to see, but the mind is not praying at all.[21]

In the measure in which one is capable of it, the Holy Spirit can stir up in the intellect inscrutable thoughts during the recollection of prayer. Prayer is interrupted, the intellect is absorbed in wonder *(tehro)*, and the object desired in prayer is forgotten. The faculties are plunged into a profound drunkenness, and humans are no more in this world:

> There is no longer any discernment of either body or soul there, or any recollection of anything. . . . No longer does the mind actually pray, but there is a gaze of wonder at the inaccessible things which do not belong to the world of mortal beings, and the mind is stilled, not having knowledge of anything here. This is the "unknowing" of which it is said, "Blessed is the person who has reached the unknowing during prayer which cannot be surpassed," as Evagrius said.[22]

Isaac compares this descent of the Spirit into the soul during prayer to the descent of the Spirit on the eucharistic bread and wine. "The memory of God suffices for the saints so that they can be suddenly, as in captivity, transported by love." When humans enjoy this state, they are in total repose of spirit and body.[23] They are in a state of total passivity in regard to the action of the Spirit.

In another passage, Isaac compares the activity of the Holy Spirit in prayer with the "overshadowing" of the Holy Spirit at the Annunciation. Although Mary is placed in a special category, in that her whole body and soul were sanctified, this "overshadowing" can have a temporary effect upon those whom the Spirit deems worthy: "The mind is snatched away in wonder as it is expanded to receive some divine revelation. As long as the divine activity overshadows his mind, such a person is exalted above the movement of the thoughts of his soul through communion with the Holy Spirit."[24]

## Conclusion

Isaac of Nineveh gives us an example of the mystic-theologian. While he presents us with an advanced method of spirituality and contemplation, his contribution is not just the fruit of his intellect but the product of his sanctity and mystical experience. He represents spiritual theory put into practice as well as the verification of theory through years of personal asceticism and contemplation. Perhaps this combination of praxis and spirituality explains his great popularity and broad influence.

As noted, his spiritual doctrine relied heavily on Evagrius of Pontus, the desert fathers and the masters of the Syriac tradition. However, Isaac's originality lies in his ability to provide rich detail from his experience. He is able to elaborate for us the ramifications of the crucifixion of the body and the ascent of the soul. He provides further insights into the gift of tears and the qualities of pure prayer. He describes for us the wonders of contemplation.

# 9

# Simon of Taibutheh

Simon of Taibutheh[1] is another witness of seventh-century east-ern Syriac spirituality. He lived in the region of lower Meso-potamia during the time of Patriarch Henanisho I. Simon was a physician who had studied Hippocrates and Galen. With this background he was conscious of the direct influence of the body on the soul and stressed that discipline of the body was essential to progress in the spiritual life. Simon died about 680.

In the writings of Simon of Taibutheh we have a spirituality influenced in many aspects by Pseudo–Dionysius. Reminiscent also of Evagrius, Simon distinguishes different levels of knowl-edge. The knowledge of visible things he calls natural knowledge or learning. The knowledge of the essences of rational and spir-itual beings is called spiritual *theoria*. The soul is instructed and molded by the various degrees of *theoria* until it reaches the First Being, who is the end of all varieties of knowledge.

## The Spiritual Life

The spiritual life consists of both the practical fulfillment of the commandments and the knowledge of the *theoria* of every created being. There are three stages: impassibility, purification and holi-ness.[2]

In the first stage human beings, through conscience, turn away from sin and with repentance weep over their past conduct. The second stage involves the work of discernment in the fulfillment of the commandments. Holiness, the final stage, is purity, which is sanctified by the word of God through the revelation of the Spirit.[3]

One then enters into spiritual *theoria*, where one sees in the mind spiritually all the visible things which are seen by others materially. One contemplates the past and present of creation and human history under the light of spiritual *theoria*. "The mind is taught and instructed to look inwardly at the spiritual natures, towards the secret power that is hidden in everything and works in everything in an incomprehensible way."[4]

*Theoria* is part of the salvific plan of the revelation of God's grace. It enables us to be liberated from the darkness of material things and to perceive the spiritual power that is at work within everything. For Simon, Christ's revelation of the Holy Trinity constitutes the Kingdom of God "within us" and is the fulfillment of our minds which were created in the image and likeness of God. The Kingdom of God in the soul is manifested in spiritual *theoria*.[5]

Simon, citing the writings of Pseudo–Dionysius, reaffirms that "divine Providence . . . holds all, deifies all, perfects all, illuminates all, and . . . by its perfect goodness penetrates all, sustains all, and infuses all with the desire of uniting with the Highest Divinity." This divine presence is in us and was implanted in the "foundation of all creation."[6]

In the Incarnation, God humbled himself to raise us from earthliness to spirituality by uniting the "divinity that is in us with the Highest Divinity." He did this so that by grace we are given the confidence to understand and know our deification and our formation in his likeness. Something of the highest Good is implanted in all creatures, so that through this good we might desire and long for the love of the Good One above all good. Simon also speaks of a ray emanating from God and of our longing for the "Light that is above all light."[7]

IMAGE OF GOD

Simon draws profound implications from the teaching that creatures and especially humans are in the "image of God." Simon claims that there is an intelligible mirror within the heart that God embedded when creating and which becomes his dwelling place. It is the bond, the link and the perfection of all natures. It becomes the dwelling place of the Spirit when we become adopted children through baptism and reflects the light of grace. We are called to purify this mirror from sinful passions so that it may be restored to its original beauty. When this purification is achieved, we will begin to see the hidden mysteries of all of creation as it can now reflect the illuminative power of the Holy Spirit:

> The soul becomes dazzled and bewildered by its beauty, and perceives the new light of grace through the light of its impassibility; and the mind becomes conscious of the past and future mysteries, sees through its light "as through a glass, darkly" the light of the next

world . . . tastes the delight of the revelations of the mysteries of God.[8]

While God is incomprehensible, in the paradox of revelation God speaks of himself through the scriptures which, through presenting God's teachings in different ways and revealing to us the various names of God, are the source of true knowledge and *theoria*. By meditating on the scriptures the mind is able to rise beyond its passibility in regard to earthly things: "Immediately after the mind has been illuminated and risen upwards, it becomes conscious of the rays of impassibility, and desires all the more earnestly to be drawn towards a divine light which has no image and towards a divine knowledge which transcends all intelligence." Possessed with divine grace, the mind will be conscious of the sublime and endless mysteries which flow from God, the "Father and Source of all the lights." The mind will absorb what it is able, which is determined by its eagerness and its progress in the spiritual exercises.[9]

The "First Good" draws every nature through the hidden desire that is implanted in every nature, and especially in rational beings, to seek the incomprehensible and to participate in its image, insofar as participation is possible.[10]

Simon believes that while *theoria* is implanted in our nature, it is partly beyond our powers. Our reasoning can only go so far, and then the mind must await in silence. "Divine *theoria* refers to the inward vision of the mind which extends, as much as it can, by grace, through an image—which in reality is no true image—towards the incomprehensible ray of the hidden Godhead."[11]

The final level is "no-knowledge," a knowledge that is higher than all knowledge and all understanding. "In this way, after a person has comprehended the power of all natures, he will have comprehended this one thing: that the hidden Essence is incomprehensible."[12]

Echoing Dionysius, Simon teaches that the "Highest Divinity" is the hidden Essence that is higher than all essences and intelligences, which can never be comprehended by any mind or intelligence, and which is high above all words.[13]

## Stages in the Monastic Life

The principles of the spiritual life described above are recapitulated by Simon when describing the stages of the monastic life. In the novitiate, the first stage involves obedience to all orders. In the second stage we are called to change all of our ways of conduct and to show gradual progress from an undisciplined nature to a disciplined nature. The third consists of the fight against the passions, which involves the fulfillment of the commandments. As a result our hearts will be made contrite, humble and pure. The fourth stage begins with the labors of discernment. By this Simon means what we have seen above, namely, to meditate so as to understand the hidden powers which work in the natures of created things and to search the meaning of the scriptures so as to become conscious of the full range of God's providence in creation. The fifth stage, as we have also seen, deals with seeking the *theoria* of incorporeal beings. And, in the sixth stage, the mind contemplates the mystery of the Godhead. Finally, in the seventh stage the mind surrenders to the action of divine love:[14]

> The sign of the coming of the grace is when the outer senses and the inner passions are at rest, and the impulses of the spirit are astir and the hidden consolation holds sway, and your eye is too pure to look at evil . . . and the angels of light will now and then come near you and fill you with joy, peace, consolation, and the revelations of the mysteries of knowledge."[15]

Simon warns that we must be totally committed in our endeavors. Otherwise, "we cannot free ourselves from any passion in which our heart delights, and with the love of which it is bound, even with thousands of stratagems of labors and tens of thousands of prayers of tears."[16]

In his psychosomatic view, Simon believes that the heart stamps our thoughts either for good or evil. Therefore, one must watch over the thoughts that arise from the heart and be able to discern those that are evil:[17] "Anyone who possesses the great virtues of fast, vigil and asceticism, but lacks a guard to his heart and his tongue, labors in vain." Simon calls a contrite and repentant heart "the master-key that opens the door to all virtues." This state is achieved through the practice of poverty, detachment from others, and humility.[18] We cannot allow our thoughts to distract us, but must be focused on our vigils and prayers. "Blessed is the one who has possessed the *theoria* of the Books (that is, the Scriptures), and has meditated upon them with understanding."[19]

BODY AND SOUL

As noted above, one of the themes in Simon's writings is the close relationship between the different faculties of the soul and the organs and senses of the body. This relationship makes the performance of the various exercises of asceticism especially necessary. Unless the will is disciplined, we are still a slave to our passions.

Affirming the view of the ancients that humans are indeed a microcosm, Simon eloquently declares,

> Consider, O discerning man, that you are the image of God and the bond of all creation, both of the heavenly and of the terrestrial beings, and whenever you bend your head to worship and glorify God, all the creations, both heavenly and terrestrial, bow their heads with you and in you to worship God; and whenever you do not worship and glorify Him, all the creations grieve over you and turn against you, and you fall from grace.[20]

Simon draws a distinction between the soul that has reached the stage where it can bear fruit and the soul that is barren. The former has replaced anxiety, uncertainty and dejectedness with calm, peace and joy in God. Through discipline, vigilance and discernment of the heart, it has removed harmful thoughts and the tendency to judge others with the love for all people. The barren soul is the one that manifests rancor, anxiety, perplexity, distress, dejectedness and perturbation, and which judges its neighbor.[21]

For Simon, truth cannot be achieved by going outside oneself, or by the words of others, or by reading. It must be experienced within.[22]

## The Ascents of the Spiritual Exercises

Simon speaks of three ascents, the last of which is perfection. The soul reaches illumination through a long and tortuous process. Simon describes a journey over mountains and hills, sea and land. He speaks of sultry and freezing winds before one reaches peace and serenity. When faced with these trials and hardships, some novices pull back; others press on and undergo severe trials. In the midst of their journey, they may suffer darkness, dejection and grief. Some are able to persevere through the practice of humility. Like Moses, they are filled with grace and illumined by the revelations of the Spirit. As a result, they gain a spiritual sight wherein they see the hidden power of God as it works within creation.[23]

Simon declares, "Blessed is the one who has traversed the sea and the land of labors, crossed them and reached the harbor of impassibility, and penetrated the plains of serenity, because while still in this world his soul dwells in the next."[24] However, Simon warns that even if one has meditated on the glories of God and been filled with joy and rapture, there is the danger of illusion, self-esteem or insanity.[25]

When we fail, it is due either to negligence, false suppositions, scorning of our neighbors, love of glory, envy, the desire to assert our will, natural inclinations or hatred. However, God's grace is always available unless we continue to ignore our conscience and do not seek to amend our lives.[26]

In the psychology to which Simon adheres, there is an inherent connection between the imagination, the mind and the intelligence. Therefore, unruly passions begin with the imagination and ultimately cloud the intelligence, leading to the blinding of our conscience.[27]

In accord with Simon's understanding of anatomy, the stomach affects our other organs, which in turn can interfere with the transmission of light from the brain to the heart. Observing the commandments, fasts and vigils can bring one's stomach and organs into harmony, thus allowing enlightenment to occur. On the other hand, a full stomach and dullness of the organs can lead to darkness, dejection and mental distraction. Simon advises not only fasting but also the consumption of "dry bread and salt sparingly, so that in addition to the opening of the channels that transmit light from the mind to the heart, the dust also which through the senses of the body settles on the wings of the brain may be wiped off."[28]

### ALTARS OF KNOWING

Again restating the major themes of the spiritual life outlined above, Simon speaks of three altars of knowing. The first is the knowledge of works or the observance of the commandments, and the second the knowledge of *theoria*, the meditation on the mysteries of God which are hidden in every work of creation. As we have seen, the scriptures are able to enlighten us in these matters. The third altar is the knowledge of hope, by which we draw near "the living altar which is Christ our hope and our God." Just as Christ was united with the Word of God "inseparably and for ever, so also the mind is united to Christ without any intermediary and for ever; and it is on this altar that a man sanctifies, glorifies and praises at all times; and it is through it that he lives, moves, feeds, sleeps, and does everything without interruption."[29]

True knowledge consists of freedom without fear as well as the disengagement from any forms of error. It is achieved through self-contempt, magnanimity, joy of heart, peace of mind, universal love and affection to all without distinction. One must keep in mind the mercy and generosity of God and meditate on his providence and his promises.[30]

As we have seen above, Simon teaches that *theoria* invests us with spiritual sight. We are able to see the hidden action and power of God within creation, especially in the higher creatures. We gain an understanding of the mysteries revealed in the scriptures. *Theoria* is achieved by impassibility and faith.[31]

The goal of all perfection is communion with God at a level beyond human knowledge. This communion begins while one is still a novice and takes place in the meditation of the mind during prayer. The communion with God consists in thanks and gratitude offered to God in the inwardness of the mind, with a simple faith which has no doubt. Simon gives a detailed description of the elements of this contemplation:

> The communion with God consists . . . in an ecstasy in the depth of the revelation of the mysteries which are both hidden and revealed in all the creation, and which are inscribed in the Books and in the promises of the Spirit, past and future; in a high *theoria* concerning the hidden nature of God and His providence, and His working in everything; in a deep understanding of the different kinds of elements, humors, powers, nature, genera and various species found in the creation; in the rapturous admiration of the various natural qualities of colors, forms, manners and habits which every nature received from the Creator at the time when its creation was fashioned, and which have been kept and handed down without change, according to the character of each nature, in the six thousand years of the course of the life of the world; in the constant contemplation of the complete humility of Christ our Redeemer, His incarnation, His admirable Economy which took place on our behalf, and the secret help which comes to us from the fulfillment of His holy commandments; in the contemplation of the ascension of our First–Fruits and our Hostage, who is worshipped and adored side by side with the Father and the Holy Spirit, in the unity of the Word from the Father . . . and in contemplation of our death [and] resurrection.[32]

One description that Simon gives of prayer explains that it is based not on knowledge or words but on an emptiness of the mind, in which one is at peace and can recollect in stillness. It involves the removal of all thoughts and a complete rejection of all cares. He advises,

> If you desire prayer, remove from the wings of your mind all the affairs of the world, together with its cares and glory . . . In time of prayer, leave in an intelligible abyss all that is and is not, and ascend in your mind naked towards the Cross, and pass over to the next world. Begin your prayer empty of everything, so that perchance you may be able to recite a serene prayer.[33]

Simon also describes prayer as an "inner vision which is illuminated by the Spirit, and which contemplates inwardly the good implanted in the heart."[34]

## Conclusion

Simon of Taibutheh, like Isaac of Nineveh, gives us an ascetical-mystical doctrine based on lived experience. Differing from those of Isaac, Simon's writings reflect the influence of Dionysius the Areopagite. God is incomprehensible but is also the ultimate Good and the "Father of Lights." God's illumination is contained in his image which is embedded in us at creation. The scriptures are a positive source of illumination. The closer we climb toward God, the stronger we are drawn by his "rays." Simon also provides practical ascetical advice to those seeking to progress in the spiritual life. With Simon we have Dionysian theory become contemplative practice.

# 10

## Dadisho Katraya

Dadisho was a Nestorian spiritual writer who lived probably in the second half of the seventh century. He was born in Bet–Katraya, a region bordering the Persian Gulf, and became a monk of the monastery of Rab–Kinnare. He died about 690. All that we know about him comes from his work. Like Isaac of Nineveh, Dadisho draws on Evagrius, the *Apophthegmata* and related literature, the *Macarian Homilies*, Abba Isaiah and Mark the Hermit, as well as on earlier Syriac writers.[1]

Dadisho's writings emphasize practical matters in the spiritual life. His main interest is with monks and ascetics. His work, *On The Solitude of Seven Weeks,* concerns especially the spiritual exercises that monks who led a cenobitic life should undertake during their retreats of seven days or seven weeks. It is an exposition of asceticism and mysticism.[2]

Dadisho believes Christ has provided us with various ways to achieve salvation so that no believing Christian will be denied the promise of the Kingdom. He describes four levels of the Christian life in ascending toward perfection. Besides the laity and the "Sons of the Covenant," there are the monks who do not marry or eat meat. They recite the Divine Office, work in the fields and offer hospitality to travelers. Beyond them are the anchorites or solitaries *(ihidaya)*. There are six classes of solitaries: the young solitaries who still live a cenobitic life; those that live in their own cells and practice the short solitude of seven days; those who keep the solitude of seven weeks; those who live alone as hermits in deserts and wastelands, but who occasionally come back for short periods to the monasteries and live with their fellowmen; itinerant solitaries who go from monastery to monastery and live in special cells outside the communal life of the brothers; and the perfect solitary or anchorite who lives apart from all human contact. The last three are solitaries strictly speaking.[3]

It is interesting to note that Dadisho refers to the "Sons of the

Covenant," which indicates that this institution still existed at his time. However, he seems to be the last author to mention them.

## Solitude of Seven Weeks

The *Solitude of Seven Weeks* speaks of exercises for the mind and body. The bodily exercises include vigils, fasts and recitation of the Divine Office. The exercises of the mind involve meditation and contemplation. The goal of these practices is to reach the level of "pure prayer" and "mystical prayer." In meditating on scripture, one is to stress especially sorrow and repentance. The ultimate state of perfection is a state of contemplation where one has overcome passion and temptation.[4]

Dadisho describes the prayer ritual in use in the time of Babai the Great. The monks went out of their cells only on a Saturday in the evening and came to the community while fasting because they received communion on Saturday evenings throughout the year. At the monastery they listened to the public reading and participated in the evening eucharistic service. After going to the refectory, they recited the final Vespers. The whole night was spent in prayer and without sleep. They recited psalms and read the works of Theodore of Mopsuestia and the Fathers of the Desert.[5]

For Dadisho, life alone in the desert is subject to three major struggles, namely, the fears that arise at night, the weariness that can set in during the day, and the delusions brought about by the devil. He warns that one who is ignorant, lacks in the love of God, does not possess endurance, or does not have a spiritual director can be in grave danger of failing.[6]

The person who seeks solitude, especially the solitude of the Seven Weeks, must have good intention, perform his spiritual services in his cell in an undisturbed silence, and have a leader. By good intention Dadisho means that one chooses solitude only for the sake of God and the love of Jesus Christ and does not expect any earthly reward for his efforts, whether it be bodily rest, promotion or glory.[7]

The young solitary must deal with excessive dejectedness and temptations regarding the passions from the devil. He needs an old and experienced director who will console him and reprove him if he has given into his passions.[8]

While the monks who live in community are called to fasts,

vigils, abstinence, recitation of psalms, frequent genuflections and sleeping on the bare ground, those who seek solitude strive for even more demanding goals. These include

1. Weeping over past sins and mourning over daily imperfections.
2. Hardening oneself against temptations.
3. Self-analysis so as to become aware of one's wrong inclinations.
4. Continuous remembrance of God and rejection of all other memories.
5. Struggling against passions and demons.
6. Purity of heart.
7. Peace of mind.
8. Pure prayer.[9]

Dadisho states that to acquire purity of heart and make one's solitude fruitful one must reach the stage of incessant prayer without distraction and acquire the ability to reject the temptations of the devil as quickly as they occur. He explains that these two virtues are beyond any of our efforts to acquire and can be bestowed only through the grace of the Holy Spirit. "They produce the following effects: a spiritual impulse which incessantly stirs the impulses of the soul with the ardor of the perfect love of God; and the sight of the light and the glory of our Lord Jesus Christ, through revelation of the Holy Spirit."[10]

In another *Discourse*, Dadisho teaches that every rational being has been created with three powers for the work of righteousness: knowledge, love and fervor. The attributes of love are "zeal, affection, desire, happiness, spiritual emotion, joy in God, delight in righteousness, longing for its fulfillment and eagerness in the expectation of its reward."[11]

> The attributes of knowledge are true faith, contemplation of God, constant direction of the mind towards our Lord Jesus Christ, spiritual understandings, meditation on righteousness, the remembrance of the mercies which God gave or promised to us, recollection of former sins and daily imperfections, reflection on the knowledge of the passions and the virtues, and self-improvement, together with the remembrance of the hour of death, Judgment, Hell, Heaven, Paradise, and similar things.[12]

The attributes of fervor are "hope in God and confidence in Him, strength against the passions, fortitude against the demons, endurance of fights, patience in tribulations, firmness in the struggle, refusal to own defeat in labors."[13]

## PASSIONS AND VIRTUES

In two further *Discourses*, Dadisho warns that there are four predominant passions that the beginning solitary must war against if he is to achieve the state of perfection and purity of heart in which he can begin contemplation and pure prayer. They are gluttony, excessive sleep, anger and vainglory. Two of them are passions of the body, and two are passions of the soul; these four are the key to defeating the other passions. Overcoming vainglory means also the overcoming of pride. The defeat of gluttony leads to unconcern for one's body and to generosity, thus subduing the love of money. Conquering gluttony, sleep and vainglory means overcoming fornication. Controlling one's passions means the diminishment of love of pleasures and thereby enables one to fight off temptations to discontent and dejectedness.[14]

Pure prayer is accomplished, performed, constituted and kept by four virtues—fasts, vigils, meekness and humility—two of which belong to the body and two to the soul. And the exercise of solitude is aimed at the practice of three virtues: faith that comes from hearing, hope, and love, through which personal faith is made manifest for the spiritual vision of our Lord.[15]

Dadisho repeats the need to practice incessant and undisturbed prayer, quick rejection of evil thoughts and endurance of all trials. Having achieved perfection through this exercise of hope and contemplation, the solitary enters on the exercise of love where he encounters the fruits of the Spirit. He especially experiences joy of the love of Christ and the Father, complete meekness, and personal faith, which is a spiritual vision of Christ through the revelation of the Holy Spirit.[16]

# 11

# Joseph and Abdisho Hazzaya

Joseph Hazzaya ("Visionary") was a Nestorian monk of the eighth century. His family had been Zoroastrians, and as a youth he had been led away into slavery. Subsequently he became a Christian, was freed by his Christian master and became a monk of the monastery of Abba Sliwa in north Iraq. After living in community as prescribed by the canons, he lived for many years in solitude. He was made head of the Monastery of Mar Bassima. He then spent a second period in solitude on Mt. Zinai in Adiabene, after which he was chosen head of the Monastery of Rabban Bokhtisho, which was close to his hermitage, and where he died at an advanced age.

Abdisho of Nisibis (d. 1318) says in his catalogue that Joseph wrote 1900 treatises and lists the titles of ten of them. Among the works that come to us are two chapters of the treatise "On Contemplation and Its Different Species" found in the *Woodbrooke Studies*. Some of his writings were circulated under the name of his brother and fellow monk, Abdisho.[1] Therefore, we are considering the writings under both names in the same chapter.

According to Robert Beulay, Joseph's writings were influenced by many predecessors. From Evagrius, whom he cites often, he took such ideas as the various types of contemplation, the distinction between body, soul and intellect, the enumeration of different colors of the soul, and the drawing of analogies from Exodus. The influence of Pseudo–Marcarius is seen in Joseph's stress that the search for God should focus on the interior of the heart, in the way he describes the action of the Spirit in the soul and how it is manifested, and in his use of the symbol of fire. From John the Solitary, Joseph employs the division of the three degrees of corporeal, psychic and spiritual; however, he takes a different approach. For John they represented various modes of life, while for Joseph they are objects of asceticism or contemplation. From John also comes the distinction between purity and limpidity or transparence and probably the relationship between the psychic degree and life in solitude. He also cites Theodore of Mopsuestia and Pseudo–Dionysius.[2]

The synod of 786–87 under Patriarch Timothy I accused Joseph of rejecting the need for prayer and the divine office in receiving the gifts of the Holy Spirit. According to Beulay, Joseph had made this statement only in regard to passive contemplative states, which are not definitive, and had recommended that when they ceased one should return to active prayer and the divine office.[3]

As implied above, the doctrine of Joseph Hazzaya is based on the division of the spiritual life into corporeal, psychic and spiritual degrees. However, he is the first author to combine with these three degrees two other elements, the division of stages of "purity," "limpidity" and "perfection" and the Evagrian approach to contemplation. This synthesis can be schematized as follows: (1) corporeal degree, beginning with purity and the contemplation of things corporeal; (2) psychic degree, beginning with limpidity and the contemplation of incorporeal things and of judgment and providence; and (3) spiritual degree, dealing with perfection, contemplation of the Holy Trinity.[4]

## Corporeal Degree

The corporeal degree corresponds to living in community. The focus of asceticism is on exercises involving the body such as fasting, vigil, voluntary poverty, exterior works of charity. Prayer is expressed through the psalms and spiritual reading. The analogy of this level is to the passage of the Israelites in the desert and to the state of a servant under the rule of the commandments. Works at this stage are accompanied by tears of joy and contrition. When one has reached a state of purification on this level, one acquires purity and is said to have achieved a "baptism of the body." In fact, Joseph sees the spiritual life as an extension of baptismal grace.[5]

Even at this first stage the soul is capable of mystical experience and can have a vision of sapphire light and of heaven. One is able also to contemplate the corporeal world and see the workings of God's providence and wisdom. Although it is mystical, this contemplation deals with material things and ideas that are less than simple. The biblical analogy is to the Israelites at the foot of Sinai. At this stage, the soul is subject to many temptations but especially those of vainglory, acedia, gluttony and lust.[6]

The writings attributed to Abdisho speak of the stages of purity, serenity and perfection. At the stage of purity, the soul strives to purify itself of its vices. Recitation of the psalms is advised along with the reading of the scriptures. With prostrations the ascetic may be granted the gift of tears, which arise from a fire that burns within the soul and signify the boundary between the stages of purity and serenity.[7]

## Psychic Stage

Joseph's psychic stage involves the practice of solitude. One is called to practice the interior virtues of humility, patience and goodness. The goal is to acquire a partial limpidity. The difference between purity and limpidity is that purity has the meaning of our original state of righteousness before sin and focuses on the exterior person while limpidity refers to total integrity extending to the very root of the interior person. At this latter level the soul contemplates incorporeal beings.[8]

At the level of partial limpidity there are combats, temptations, vicissitudes and sometimes the feeling of being abandoned by God. It constitutes the baptism of the soul and is analogous to the state of being a son. The transition from the stage of the body to that of the soul corresponds to the crossing by the Israelites of the river Jordan. The ensuing fight with demons reflects the Israelites' fight with the inhabitants of the Promised Land.[9]

After the combats at the beginning of the psychic stage, the soul beholds itself as a crystalline light. The writings attributed to Abdisho also claim that in true serenity the mind receives *theoria* in the image of a crystal light, where it contemplates spiritual beings who in their fiery nature constantly give glory to the Triune and incomprehensible God.[10]

Joseph goes on to say that at that stage the mind contemplates incorporeal things and God's judgment and providence. The ascetic is filled with love for all persons. One learns of the divine plan of salvation and experiences incessant tears of admiration and joy. However, the soul may still be ensnared by false suggestions from the devil.[11]

Abdisho's description of the sphere of serenity is identical. Mental prayer consists in the contemplation of the presence and workings of God's wisdom in creation. The soul is filled with the love of all persons and with a continual prayer for their conversion. One experiences peace and quiet. Through immaterial impulses which are hidden in the natures of created things, the soul is attracted to an understanding of God's providence and judgments in an experience of ecstasy, where all its faculties cease to function.[12]

Writing on spiritual prayer, Joseph Hazzaya says,

> The sphere where spiritual prayer is prayed by the mind is the mind's natural sphere: once the mind has reached that pure sphere which belongs to its true nature, once its vision has been clarified of all the imaginings and images of thoughts which do not belong to its true nature, and once the mind has been held worthy of an illuminated vision of its own self, and there has arisen within it the visionary spirit that gives insight into spiritual understanding of both corporeal and incorporeal beings, and at the same time, of Judgment and providence—it is at that point that the mind prays with spiritual prayer, a kind of prayer that is not prayed with the body's senses, but with the inner impulses of the soul which are entirely filled with illumination. Then the mind can see the birth of things past, present, and future, as well as the varied ordering of the worlds.[13]

For Abdisho, our minds experience through the Holy Spirit, whom they have received in baptism, "the power of the treasure of life which is found within them." They experience in a vision an understanding of the depths of all of creation. When they approach interior prayer, "a fiery impulse stretches in their soul, which exhales sweet odor, the perfume of which is ineffable."[14]

As a result of this impulse, the mind experiences light, truth, certainty, an understanding of incorporeal things and a consciousness of the next world. The soul is taken beyond its own nature and approaches impassibility. This impulse opens the inner door of the heart and reveals the place in which Christ resides. If this contemplative experience continues, the spiritual *theoria* "will shine in the soul like a luminous cloud, on the vision and the understanding of the past and future worlds: . . .and the mind will have no other feeling but that of its vision and its understanding."[15]

According to the writings attributed to Abdisho, the signs of the working of the Spirit are burning love of God, humility, kindness to all persons, remembrance of God alone and "the illuminated vision of your mind, which is seen in the firmament of your heart like the sapphire sky."[16]

For Joseph, at the stage of total limpidity one contemplates through a vision, which is a direct apprehension of the light or of the action of God in our created natures. It is analogous to Jerusalem, the promised land, the place free from passions of the soul and body in a light of impassibility. It is the vision of worlds which were and are, the burning stupor of love before the divine light that penetrates all and wherein the spirit no longer distinguishes itself from the light. Joseph considers spiritual contemplation to be an intermediary between the psychic and the spiritual stage.[17]

## Spiritual Stage

The spiritual level or stage of perfection is beyond the action of the senses or the soul. It is on the level of the intellect, a "baptism of the intellect." Incorporeal powers are seen with their natures totally penetrated by the light of the Holy Trinity. In a continual stupor, the spirit comes to an understanding of the "holy, holy, holy" uttered by incorporeal beings. It has a vision of formless light of the Trinity and of Christ in his resurrected glory. The soul appears as fire or the sun but is not able in fact to distinguish its being from the formless light which shines. This contemplation is inexpressible, for it consists in simple and unlimited movements of the soul. This final stage is analogous to the heavenly Zion where there are no more tears.[18]

Abdisho declares that at the sphere of spirituality the mind no longer contemplates with image or likeness but experiences a single vision of light. At this stage the mind no longer knows itself nor can it distinguish itself from the light which has absorbed it. "There will be neither thought of anything, nor any impulses and inward movements, but only ecstasy in God and an ineffable rapture." In this sphere of perfection no prayers and sacrifices are offered. One even ceases to remember former acts of prayer.[19]

According to Abdisho, although the scriptures portray God in images so that he might reveal himself to us, God is beyond image and likeness. His true nature cannot be represented because he is finer than the fire, light and air of which even the higher creatures are composed. Even the divine light we experience is unlike any created light.[20]

Beulay claims that in this teaching on the vision of God Joseph seems to combine two influences: that of Evagrius (among others), for whom this vision takes place in the mirror of the soul (or in the heart, according to Macarian tradition); and that of Nestorian theology (inherited from the school of Antioch) for which there can be no direct contemplation of God, who is absolutely invisible in himself, but for which the vision takes place only through the mediation of the visible humanity of Christ.[21]

# 12

# John of Dalyatha (John Saba)

John of Dalyatha or John Saba is the last representative we are
citing from the Syriac spiritual tradition. Much in John's writings
had already been developed by earlier teachers. We see in him
influences from John the Solitary, Pseudo–Macarius, Evagrius
and Pseudo–Dionysius, among others. Nevertheless, he offers
his own insights, especially in the intensity with which he describes mystical experiences. We also learn a little more about the
nature of prayer, pure prayer and its relationship to the spiritual
concept of limpidity or lucidity of heart.

John of Dalyatha was a hermit and Nestorian of the eighth
century. He was born in what is today north Iraq and was a monk
during the first two-thirds of the century, at first in Qardu (south-
east modern Turkey) and later in the mountains of Dalyatha to the
east of Qardu.

His most important writings consist of twenty-two homilies or
discourses and a collection of fifty-one short letters. John's writings were condemned by Patriarch Timothy of the Church of the
East at a synod in 786/87 for showing Messalian tendencies.[1] The
Nestorian church apparently grouped under the umbrella of Messalianism any claim that the Divinity can be experienced directly
whether in a sensible or corporeal fashion, as the Messalians
seemed to have asserted, or in the spiritual vision claimed by the
mystics. This position is due perhaps to the doctrinal teaching of
the Church of the East affected by Nestorian thought that even
the human Christ could not directly see his Divinity.[2]

However, John's writings were admired by succeeding genera-
tions of Syriac monks, both eastern and western. He is cited often
by Bar Hebraeus. His works were translated both into Arabic (in
which he is known as "the Spiritual Sheikh") and, in part, into
Greek. The writings under the name of John Saba are his. John
Saba appears as an intuitive and enthusiastic mystic, without too
much culture, who writes in a style that is often chaotic but full of
the fire of a dazzling spiritual experience.[3]

Like others in the Syriac tradition, John attempts to arrange the

spiritual life into the stages of corporeal, psychic and spiritual. There is an Evagrian influence, but it is apparent only along general lines. John of Dalyatha sees the mystic as "the anticipated resurrection," the fruit of baptism and of the eucharist. The importance he gives these two sacraments belies the charge of Messalianism. He also teaches that the demon is unable to penetrate to the interior of a person.[4]

Like others, John of Dalyatha stresses the need for the virtue of humility so that one's thoughts are to be considered as "less than dust and ashes." One should also strive for the gift of tears, and for a repentance that gives birth to purity and illumination. One must practice good deeds towards others, have pity for the oppressed and minister to the sick.[5]

PRAYER

Prayer for John is in stages. First, the "prayer of movements," that which "consists in knocking at the door of the Giver." An intermediate form of prayer seems to be the practice of "the remembrance of God." It involves an interior and simple movement which causes all "movements" to cease and consists in "persevering without support at the door of the heart" and "to fix continually one's spiritual gaze on the interior up to seeing the beauty of the Lordship of Christ in the interior man." The third stage is "the entrance into the place of mysteries" and the passive experience of wonder caused by God. This is no longer prayer as such, and John sometimes refers to it as "true prayer" or "the perfection of prayer." Since it is brought about by the work of the Spirit in us, it is beyond our power. It is "continual prayer which is stupor before God."[6]

John describes the stage of perfection as entering into a treasury, a place of revelations, of joy and of light, where "inhabitants are illuminated by the sight of the beauty of the king."[7] He goes further and speaks about "fiery impulses" aroused by the Spirit:

Sometimes it [namely, the Spirit or "Grace"] stirs up hot fiery impulses in his heart through the love of Christ and his soul is set on fire, his limbs are paralyzed and he falls on his face. Sometimes it arouses a fervent heat in his heart and his body and soul are enkindled so that he supposes that every part of him is consumed by the conflagration, except what is in his heart.[8]

PURITY OF HEART

Sebastian Brock points out that Syriac writers used the term "lucidity of heart" as another way to describe "purity of heart." Lucidity can also be defined as limpidity, clarity and sincerity. In the later Syriac writers "lucidity of heart" is stressed constantly as the prerequisite for pure prayer. John is quoted as saying, "The heart should be entirely lucid." Lucidity of heart provides the means for God's self-revelation to humanity.[9]

Like other Syriac writers John understands human beings to be created in the image and likeness of God. Their souls were intended to be a mirror reflecting God's presence and the light of his glory. This image has been distorted by sin and must be purified by ascetical works and the Spirit of God that we receive in baptism.

John teaches that once the heart has achieved purity, it can again behold God's "ineffable radiance and wondrous beauty," fulfilling the beatitude, "Blessed are those who are pure in their heart, for they shall see God" (Letter 14.1–2). John further explains that if we purify the mirror of our heart we will experience "the Triune Light" and the reality of God (Letter 28.2).[10] John declares,

> You are the image of God, O man. Do you wish the image to take on the Likeness of its Model? Then silence all activity of any kind and carry the yoke of your Lord in your heart and wonder at his majesty in your mind continuously, until the image becomes resplendent with his glory, and it is transformed into the Likeness, and you shall become in God a god who has acquired the likeness of his Maker by means of the union which makes like to himself. (Letter 29.1)[11]

John pursues this idea of union with God or divinization by drawing an example of the making of iron. He explains that in the process fire and iron become one. The iron in the furnace takes on the likeness of the fire; there is only one image while the two substances remain separate. "In the same way the children of God see themselves as the image of God; so they all become gods by the grace of their creator."[12]

# Appendix: Stephen Bar Sudaili

As mentioned in the foreword, we are including this summary of the thought of Stephen Bar Sudaili in an appendix. Although originating from a Syriac milieu, Stephen chose for his spiritual masters Origen and Evagrius of Pontus. But, more than any other Syriac writer, Stephen took the writings of Origen and Evagrius to their extreme conclusions, to the point where they were obviously heretical. Since he does not offer an accurate witness to the development of Syriac spirituality, we thought it would not be warranted to place him in the main body of the text.

Our principal source about the life of Stephen Bar Sudaili (born c. 500) is Philoxenus of Mabboug, who wrote against the Origenist errors to be found in Stephen's writings. We have additional details from other Syriac writers. Stephen was a monk who originated in Edessa. He was still young when James of Serug (d. 521) sent him a letter which, while praising his zeal and piety, reprimanded him for opinions about the limited duration of the punishments of hell and of the rewards of heaven. Being accused of heresy, he left his native country and went to the region of Jerusalem where Origenist monks resided. He may have returned to Edessa and died there shortly after 543.

As mentioned above, Stephen Bar Sudaili was influenced not only by the Origenist tradition but especially by Evagrius. Origen had claimed that movement is the cause of evil and leads to *agnosia* (lack of knowledge). It is the climb towards *gnosis* (knowledge) that leads back to God.[1] According to Philoxenus, Stephen's errors consisted of claiming that all beings were once of one substance with God, that movement is due to the primordial fall of rational creatures, and that at the end of the world all things will become identical with God.

Philoxenus reproaches Stephen for having adopted the ideas of Jewish millenarians in placing after the resurrection two successive retributions that he called "repose or liberty" and "perfection or divinity." This concept rests on a mystical interpretation of the days of the week, this present world being Friday or the sixth day, the "repose" being Saturday, and the consummation being

Sunday, the first or the eighth day. In the period of repose the just enjoy the promised rewards and the impious are subjected to chastisement for their faults, of such a sort that Christ ends by being "all in all." After repose comes the consummation of eternity, when "God will be all in all." All creatures, including the demons, will be only one substance with him. All distinctions will cease, to the point that the distinction even of three divine Persons will be abolished.

### Book of the Holy Hierotheos

Stephen is the author of the *Book of the Holy Hierotheos*. Although this book claims as its master the teacher of Pseudo–Dionysius, Irenée Hausherr and others claim that its composition, at least under the form that we have, was done after the date of the Pseudo–Dionysian writings and was based on Evagrius. Influences from Pseudo–Dionysius are peripheral; they were introduced once the basic thought was already there.

Hausherr has shown that the *Book of the Holy Hierotheos* did not exercise the influence on Isaac of Nineveh that F. S. Marsh believed. The book gives us an example of the extreme in spirituality to which the teachings of Origen could be taken.[2] Hausherr claims that it was non-existent in the East and not easy to find in the West up to the thirteenth century.[3]

The *Book of the Holy Hierotheos* is divided into five parts: the first deals with cosmology; the next three with the ascent of the intellect toward its perfection; and the fifth with eschatology. It tends to be very esoteric.

Stephen claims that at one time rational beings were incorporeal and of one substance with the Divine. The intellect, because of its negligence, has gone outside its nature and fallen. This has brought about the "first movement" or a "descending" movement and led to the distinction among beings. As a result of this fall, we have the creation of the soul ("the vestment of the intellect") and the body ("the house of the soul").[4]

One achieves salvation by ascending toward God through knowledge. In the course of its ascension, described especially in the middle parts of the book, the intellect is assailed successively by three demonic entities, which are found at different levels between heaven and earth. Having arrived above the firmament, it is guided by the angels who, at various levels, are as the "guardians of the House of God." The intellect is raised from dwelling place to dwelling place, nourished in each by a mysterious, mystical bread that ignites in it the desire to progress always toward the Good. Then the intellect undergoes a mystical crucifixion so that it might be further purified. This is the mystical death of the intellect.[5]

After passing three days in the tomb, the intellect experiences a mystical resurrection and returns to life in body and soul which, now purified, are rendered brilliant and realize their complete unification with the intellect. All the evil that remains regroups and takes the form of a great Tree against which the intellect must battle. It breaks and cuts the branches in vain, for the Tree always sprouts back. The intellect finds that it is necessary to take out the roots. To achieve this it must redescend, which it does with suffering and tears. In the course of its new voyage, the intellect again passes by the firmament and the earth and then moves under the earth. There it is assailed by demons and would succumb if Christ, the great intellect, did not come to its aid. Carried along with him, it regains the heights (that is, a second ascension) and is informed that the Tree of Evil is annihilated.[6]

SECOND BAPTISM

Stephen Bar Sudaili teaches the necessity of baptism to be saved. But there is, beyond the baptism of water, a "second baptism" that the intellect ought to receive above the heavens. Only the baptism of the spirit and of fire, of which baptism of water is merely the symbol, is able to realize the union with the Good. After this baptism, in the course of which the Spirit has descended on it, the intellect becomes equal to Christ to the point that it lays aside the name of "intellect" and is called henceforth simply "Christ."[7]

Having become Christ, the intellect reigns over all those that are still in the body and attains the function that most belongs to Christ, which is to consecrate. It enters the Holy of Holies to accomplish the mystical sacrifice and to distribute the eucharist to the angels. This mystical bread is none other than perfect knowledge, of which the intellect has become worthy and which it communicates with those who are above it. The eucharistic bread here below is only the symbol of this heavenly eucharistic bread. The same applies to the wine. The author explains that the eucharist with material bread is appropriate for those living still in the body, while their intellect already partakes of the celestial sacrament.[8]

Having reached paradise, spiritually speaking, the intellect finds the Tree of Life, whose vision is "the accomplishment of all vision and the term of mystery." The intellect is seduced for a moment by a false nature which takes the appearance of a "Tree of Life." It is liberated by Christ, who destroys this fallacious nature and leads the intellect towards the true Tree of Life. Then the mystic Sword appears to the intellect, which is invited to take it and to descend anew to combat the demons. This new descent is made with joy, and the intellect retraces its steps, traversing the firmament and the guardian angels. At the gates of the Abyss, it combats the demons and is triumphant. It appears to them as a brilliant light, and these fallen intellects see their shadows dissipated. The inferior regions are filled with light, and the demons of hell beg the intellect to have pity and to unite them to it.[9]

TRANSFIGURATION

The intellect then climbs triumphantly and proclaims the resurrection. The intellect now knows no limit. It lays aside even the name "Christ," for it henceforth has no name at all. The perfect intellect moves beyond love, for the latter still supposes a distinction between the subject who loves and the object loved. According to the *Book of Holy Hierotheos, teoria,* or contemplation, goes beyond vision and image. It creates a New World and a New Person in its own image without image, and in its own likeness without likeness. This transfiguration, this fusion into divine power, would thus be experienced in a state in which the object is neither seen nor heard but is most intensely felt as present.[10]

The *Book of Holy Hierotheos* declares,

Those minds, therefore, that have been accounted worthy of perfection no longer have either affection or love; for they leave behind them every name that is used as distinct and indicating something, and now become nameless above name, and speechless above speech.[11]

The intellect even abandons the name of "Divinity." These divinized intellects are above union, for one no longer speaks of "union" but of "mixture"; the word "union" still implies a certain distinction between those who are united.[12] The author writes, ". . . Just as the ray shining through the window is not a ray when it is commingled with its Essence, so the mind is no longer the mind when it is commingled with God."[13] The ascent of contemplation goes from the stage of love and affection, in which distinction still exists, to the stage of unification, in which distinction begins to fade, to the final state of commingling.

In mixture there is no longer any distinction. There are intellects that have arrived above union. This distinction between "union" and "mixture" is not found in Origen or Evagrius. Hausherr believes Stephen got the idea from Pseudo–Dionysius, for whom divinity is above union itself.[14]

In this fifth part of *Hierotheos*, Stephen claims that nothing is abolished but all is destined to be restored, reunited and mixed in the Father, such that there will be accomplished the Word: "God will be all in all." Hell will pass, punishments will end, the demons will receive grace, and the condemned will be pardoned. The angelic functions with all the hierarchies will cease, and all distinction will disappear.[15]

All shall be absorbed in unity. Names will be erased to the point that "God himself will pass, Christ will be abolished, and the Spirit will no more be called Spirit." Such shall be the consummation of all.[16]

## Conclusion

With Stephen Bar Sudaili we have a spiritual pantheism. With the premise that our souls once pre-existed in a union in knowledge with God, he can claim that the goal of the spiritual life is a restoration of that primordial union. But the price is too high. Movement is seen as a symptom of sin; material creation and the body are seen as the result of sin. The goal of existence is that creation, including the demons, be ultimately restored and unified with God. All of these ideas have been condemned by the Church's councils as being outside biblical teaching and the Christian tradition. While Stephen's analysis of the progress of the intellect toward purification and perfection may offer some provocative insights, Stephen's vision is so blurred by erroneous presumptions as to confuse and mislead the reader.

# Notes

## Chapter 1. Early Developments: Ephrem and Aphraat

1. Cited in Brock, *The Luminous Eye* (Rome: C.I.I.S. Publications, 1985), 29–30.

2. Ibid., 14–15.

3. Hausherr, "Aphraat," *Dictionnaire de Spiritualité* 1 (Paris: Beauchesne, 1937): cols. 746–47.

4. Nedungatt, "The Covenanters of the Early Syriac–Speaking Church," *Orientalia Christiana Periodica* 39 (Rome: Pontificium Institutum Orientalium Studiorum, 1973): 192–93.

5. Cited in Ibid., 438.

6. Murray, "The Exhortation to Candidates for Ascetical Vows at Baptism in the Ancient Syriac Church," *New Testament Studies* 21 (Cambridge: Cambridge University Press, 1974): 67.

7. Murray, *Symbols of Church and Kingdom* (Cambridge: Cambridge University Press, 1975), 13–17.

8. Cited in Murray, "Exhortation to Candidates . . . ," 65–66.

9. Baker, "Syriac and the Origins of Monasticism," *Downside Review* 86 (Downside, England: St. Gregory's Society, 1968): 401.

10. Gribomont, "Monasticism and Asceticism: Eastern Christianity," *Christian Spirituality: Origins to the Twelfth Century*, Bernard McGinn, John Meyendorff and Jean Leclercq, eds. (New York: Crossroad, 1987), 90.

11. Murray, "Exhortation to Candidates," 72–73, 75.

12. Drijvers, "Hellenistic and Oriental Origins," *The Byzantine Saint*, Sergei Hackel, ed. *Studies Supplementary to Sobornost* 5 (London: Fellowship of St. Alban and St. Sergius, 1981): 31–33.

13. Baker, "Origins of Monasticism," 349–50.

14. Beck, "Asceticisme et Monachisme chez St. Éphrem," *L'Orient Syrien* 3 (1958): 277.

15. Murray, "Exhortation to Candidates," 69.

16. Nedungatt, "Covenanters of the Holy Spirit," 203–4.

17. Jargy, "Les 'fils et filles du pacte' dans la littérature monastique syriaque," *Orientalia Christiana Periodica* 17 (Rome: Pontificium Institutum Orientalium Studiorum, 1951): 318–20.

18. Murray, "Exhortation to Candidates," 69.

19. Brock, "Early Syrian Asceticism," *Numen* 20 (Leiden: Bril, 1973): 11–13.

20. Voobus, *History of Asceticism in the Syrian Orient* (Corpus Scriptorum Christianorum Orientalium 197, Subsidia, Tome 17 (Louvain: Secretariat du Corpus SCO, 1960): 256, 278–83.

21. Ibid., 309–12.

22. Nedungatt, "Covenanters of the Holy Spirit," 425–27.

23. Hausherr, "Aphraat," cols. 748–50.

24. Leloir, "La pensée monastique d'Ephrem et Martyrius," *Orientalia Christiana Analecta* 197 (Rome: Pontificium Institutum Orientalium Studiorum, 1974): 112.

25. Ibid., 112–16, 32–34.

26. Ibid., 118.

27. Ibid., 118–20.

28. Cited in Brock, "The Prayer of the Heart in Syriac Tradition," *Sobornost* 4:2 (London: Fellowship of St. Alban and St. Sergius, 1982): 134.

29. Brock, *The Syriac Fathers on Prayer and the Spiritual Life* (Kalamazoo, Mich.: Cistercian Publications, 1987), 5.

30. Brock, "Prayer of the Heart," 140.

31. Brock, "Ephrem's Letter to Publius," *Le Muséon* 89 (Louvain: Societé des Lettres et des Sciences, 1976): 286.

32. Cited in Brock, *Luminous Eye*, 56–57.

33. Ibid., 104.

34. Brock, *Syriac Fathers*, 34–36.

35. Hausherr, "Les grandes courants de la spiritualité orientale," *Orientalia Christiana Periodica* 1 (Rome: Pontificium Institutum Orientalium Studiorum, 1935): 119–20.

36. Hausherr, "Aphraat," cols. 750–52.

37. Voobus, "The Institution of the Benai Qeiama and Benat Qeiama in the Ancient Syrian Church," *Church History* 30 (Scottsdale, Pa.: American Society of Church History, 1961): 19.

38. Leloir, "La Pensée Monastique," 132.

39. Gribomont, "Le monachisme au sein de l'Église en Syrie et en Cappadoce," *Studia Monastica* 7 (Barcelona: Abadia de Montserrat, 1965): 8–12, 17.

40. It should be recalled that already in the fourth century the church declared against those who had condemned marriage, such as Marcion and the Acts of Judas Thomas. The clearest statement was by the Council of Gangra in Cappadocia in 351. That synod, assembled by Eusebius of Nicomedia, condemned those who frowned upon such institutions as marriage, family, social order and the clergy. Gribomont, "Monasticism and Asceticism: Eastern Christianity," *Christian Spirituality: Origins to the Twelfth Century*, B. McGinn, J. Meyendorff and J. Leclercq, eds. (New York: Crossroad, 1987): 91.

41. Murray, "The Features of the Earliest Christian Asceticism," *Christian Spirituality: Essays in Honor of E. Gordon Rupp*, P. Brooks ed. (London: S. C. M. Press, 1975): 71–72. See also Beck, "Asceticisme et Monachisme," 282.

42. Murray, "Earliest Christian Asceticism," 66–68.

## Chapter 2. *Liber Graduum* (Book of Degrees or Steps)

1. Baker, "The 'Gospel of Thomas' and the Syriac 'Liber Graduum,'" *New Testament Studies* 12 (Cambridge, England: Cambridge University Press, 1965–66): 49–55.

2. Baker, "Early Syriac Asceticism," *Downside Review* 88 (Downside, England: St. Gregory's Society, 1970): 393–409.

3. A. Guillaumont, "Situation et signification du 'Liber Graduum' dans la spiritualité syriaque," *Orientalia Christiana Analecta* 197 (Rome: Pontificium Institutum Orientalium Studiorum, 1974): 312 (cf. 311–26).

4. Brock, *Syriac Fathers*, 45.

5. Ibid., 54.
6. A. Guillaumont, "Liber Graduum," *Dictionnaire de Spiritualité* 9 (Paris: Beauchesne, 1976): cols. 749–52; and A. Guillaumont, "Situation et signification," 312–15.
7. A. Guillaumont, "Liber Graduum," cols. 752–54.
8. Baker, "Early Syriac Asceticism," 406.
9. Gribomont, "Monachisme au sein," 18–19.
10. Brock, *Syriac Fathers*, 46–49.

## Chapter 3. John the Solitary

1. Sebastian Brock places him in the first half of the fifth century. Brock, *Syriac Fathers*, 77.
2. Bradley, "Jean le Solitaire," *Dictionnaire de Spiritualité* 8 (Paris: Beauchesne, 1974): cols. 766–67.
3. Ibid., cols. 767–68.
4. Ibid., col. 768.
5. Ibid.
6. Hausherr, "Un grand auteur spirituel retrouvé: Jean d'Apamée," *Orientalia Christiana Analecta* 183 (Rome: Pontificium Institutum Orientalium Studiorum, 1969): 187–216.
7. Bradley, "Jean le Solitaire," cols. 768–69.
8. Ibid.
9. Harb, "Doctrine spirituelle de Jean le Solitaire (Jean d'Apamée)," *Parole de l'Orient* 2 (Kaslik, Lebanon: Université Saint–Esprit, 1971): 229–32.
10. Brock, "*Syriac Fathers*," 79.
11. Bradley, "Jean le Solitaire," col. 769.
12. Ibid., cols. 769–70.
13. Harb, "Doctrine spirituelle," 240.
14. Hausherr, "Un grand auteur," 186–216.
15. Harb, "Doctrine spirituelle," 233–36.
16. Ibid.
17. Ibid., 248–51.
18. Bradley, "Jean le Solitaire," cols. 770–71.
19. Harb, "Doctrine spirituelle," 244, 254.
20. Brock, *Syriac Fathers*, 80.
21. Harb, "Doctrine spirituelle," 259.
22. Brock, "John the Solitary, On Prayer," *Journal of Theological Studies* 30 (London: Macmillan, 1979): 99.
23. Ibid., 86–87.
24. Ibid., 97.
25. Ibid., 87.

## Chapter 4. Evagrius of Pontus

1. Bardy, "Apatheia," *Dictionnaire de Spiritualité* 1 (Paris: Beauchesne, 1937): col. 735.
2. *Acedia* has the meaning of an ennui which prevents the soul from carrying out its obligations. See Bardy, "Acedia," *Dictionnaire de Spiritualité* 1 (Paris: Beauchesne, 1937): cols. 166–68.

3. A. and C. Guillaumont, "Évagre le Pontique," *Dictionnaire de Spiritualité* 4 (Paris: Beauchesne, 1960): col. 1738.

4. Evagrius actually makes a generic distinction between the stage of *praktiké* and the stage of *gnostiké* or contemplation. *Gnostiké* is further subdivided into the contemplation of created things and *theologia* or the contemplation of the Trinity. However, for purposes of clarity we will use the term *gnosis* in reference only to the second stage.

5. Lemaitre, Roques and Viller, "Contemplation Chez les Orientaux Chrétiens," *Dictionnaire de Spiritualité* 2 (Paris: Beauchesne, 1953): cols. 1818–22.

6. Ibid., cols. 1816–17.

7. Ibid., cols. 1777–84. See also Kirchmeyer, "Extase Chez les Pères de l'Église," *Dictionnaire de Spiritualité* 4:2 (Paris: Beauchesne, 1961): col. 2099.

## Chapter 5. Philoxenus of Mabboug

1. Corless, "The Place of Syrian Christian Mysticism in Religious History," *Journal of Religious History* 5 (Sydney, Australia: University of Sydney, 1968): 6–7.

2. Brock, *Syriac Fathers*, 102–103.

3. Hausherr, "Contemplation et Sainteté, une remarqueable mise au point par Philoxène de Mabboug (+523)," *Revue d'Ascètique et de Mystique* 14 (Toulouse, France: 1933): 174.

4. Cited in Hausherr, ibid., 175.

5. Harb, "L'attitude de Philoxène de Mabboug à l'égard de la spiritualité 'savante' d'Évagre le Pontique," *Mémorial Mgr. Gabriel Khouri–Sarkis* (Louvain: Imprimerie Orientaliste, 1969): 142–49.

6. Harb, "L'attitude de Philoxène," 135–38, 142–50.

7. Lemoine, "La spiritualité de Philoxène de Mabboug," *L'Orient Syrien* 2 (Paris: 1957): 351.

8. Harb, "Les origines de la doctrine de 'la-hasusuta' (Apatheia) chez Philoxène de Mabboug," *Parole de l'Orient* 5 (Kaslik, Lebanon: Université Saint–Esprit, 1974): 230.

9. Hausherr, "Contemplation et Sainteté," 178–81.

10. Harb, "Les origines," 234–35.

11. Ibid., 236–40.

12. Cited in Hausherr, "Contemplation et Sainteté," 184.

13. Ibid.

14. Harb, "Les origines," 227–42.

15. Hausherr, "Contemplation et Sainteté," 194.

16. Harb, "L'attitude de Philoxène," 139.

17. Brock, *Syriac Fathers*, 130–31.

18. Spidlik, *La Spiritualité de L'Orient Chrétien*, Orientalia Christiana Analecta 206 (Rome: Pontificium Institutum Orientalium Studiorum, 1978): 328.

## Chapter 6. Pseudo–Dionysius the Areopagite

1. Hausherr, "Les grands courants," 124–25.

2. Rayez, "Denys l'Aréopagite: Influence du Pseudo–Denys en Orient," *Dictionnaire de Spiritualité* 3 (Paris: Beauchesne, 1957): cols. 286–318.

3. Cf. also Campbell, *Dionysius the Pseudo–Areopagite: the Ecclesiastical Hierarchy* (Washington, D.C.: Catholic University of America Press, 1955): xx–xxi.

4. Pseudo–Dionysius, *The Complete Works*, Colm Luibheid, trans. (Mahwah, N.J.: Paulist Press, 1987): 154.

5. Roques, "Dionysius l'Aréopagite," *Dictionnaire de Spiritualité* 3 (Paris: Beauchesne, 1957): cols. 260–86.

6. Roques in preface to Pseudo-Dionysius, *Complete Works*, 6.

7. Gilson, *History of Christian Philosophy in the Middle Ages* (New York: Random House, 1955), 82–85.

8. Spearritt, *A Philosophical Enquiry into Dionysian Mysticism* (Fribourg: University of Fribourg, 1968), Dissertation, passim.

9. Pseudo–Dionysius, *Complete Works*, 49.

10. Lossky, *The Mystical Theology of the Eastern Church* (Crestwood, N.Y.: St. Vladimir's Seminary, 1976), 40.

11. Roques, "Dionysius l'Aréopagite," cols. 260–86.

12. Camelot, "Lumière: Étude Patristique," *Dictionnaire de Spiritualité* 9 (Paris: Beauchesne, 1976): cols. 1155–56.

13. Spearritt, *Philosophical Enquiry*, passim.

14. Lemaitre, Roques and Villier, "Contemplation Chez les Orientaux Chrétiens, *Dictionnaire de Spiritualité* 2 (Paris: Beauchesne, 1953): cols. 1785 ff.

15. Kirchmeyer, "Extase Chez les Pères," cols. 1894–99.

16. Lossky, *Mystical Theology,* 37–38.

17. Blasucci, "Images et Contemplation," *Dictionnaire de Spiritualité* 7 (Paris: Beauchesne, 1971): cols. 1479 ff.

18. Hausherr, "Les grands courants," 124–25.

19. Kirchmeyer, "Extase Chez les Pères," cols. 1894–1905.

20. Ibid., cols. 1885–1905.

21. Pseudo–Dionysius, *Complete Works*, 80.

22. Camelot, "Lumière," ibid.

23. Kirchmeyer, "Extase Chez les Pères," cols. 1908–11.

24. Spearritt, *Philosophical Enquiry*, 153–55.

25. Pseudo–Dionysius, *The Divine Names*, in Pseudo–Dionysius, *Complete Works*, 109.

# Chapter 7. Martyrius *(Sahdona)*

1. Leloir, "La pensée monastique," 125.

2. Leloir, "Martyrius (Sahdona)," *Dictionnaire de Spiritualité* 10 (1980): cols. 741–42.

3. Ibid., col. 738.

4. Ibid.

5. Ibid., cols. 738–39.

6. Brock, *The Syriac Fathers on Prayer and the Spiritual Life* (Kalamazoo, Mich.: Cistercian Publications, Inc.): 200–201.

7. Leloir, "Martyrius (Sahdona)," col. 740.

8. Brock, *Syriac Fathers*, 202.

9. Ibid., 202–3.

10. Ibid., 210–11.

11. Ibid., 207.

12. Leloir, "Martyrius (Sahdona)," col. 741.

13. Ibid., col. 740.

14. Brock, *Syriac Fathers*, 202.

15. Leloir, "Martyrius (Sahdona)," col. 740.

16. Ibid., col. 741.
17. Brock, *Syriac Fathers*, 225.
18. Ibid., 225–28.
19. Ibid., 228.

## Chapter 8.　Isaac of Nineveh

1. Cf. Wensinck, *Mystic Treatises by Isaac of Nineveh* (Amsterdam: 1923).
2. Brock, *Syriac Fathers*, 244–45.
3. Khalifé-Hachem, "Isaac de Ninive," *Dictionnaire de Spiritualité* 7 (Paris: Beauchesne, 1951): cols. 2041–43.
4. Ibid., col. 2043.
5. Brock, "Divine Call and Human Response: The Syriac Tradition II: St. Isaac of Nineveh," *The Way* (London: The Way Publications, Jan., 1981): 68–69.
6. Khalifé-Hachem, "Isaac de Ninive," cols. 2044–45.
7. Brock, "Divine Call," 71.
8. Brock, *Syriac Fathers*, 248–49.
9. Brock, "Divine Call," 71–72.
10. Khalifé-Hachem, "Isaac de Ninive," cols. 2043–46.
11. Brock, "Divine Call," 69.
12. Ibid., 69–70.
13. Khalifé-Hachem, "Isaac de Ninive," col. 2047.
14. Ibid.
15. Ibid., cols. 2047–48.
16. Brock, "Divine Call," 74.
17. Ibid., 73.
18. Brock, *Syriac Fathers*, 253–54.
19. Khalifé-Hachem, "Isaac de Ninive," col. 2048.
20. Ibid., col. 2049.
21. Brock, *Syriac Fathers*, 254.
22. Ibid., 262–63.
23. Khalifé-Hachem, "Isaac de Ninive," cols. 2042–50.
24. Brock, "Divine Call," 73.

## Chapter 9.　Simon of Taibutheh

1. The term *taibutheh* means "his grace" and refers to the fact that Simon claimed that all things are accomplished by God's grace.
2. Simon of Taibutheh, *Mystical Works of Simon of Taibutheh*, in *Woodbrooke Studies* 7 A. Mingana, trans. (Cambridge: W. Heffer and Sons, Ltd., 1934): 13.
3. Ibid., 13–14.
4. Ibid., 14.
5. Ibid., 12.
6. Ibid.
7. Ibid., 16.
8. Ibid., 60–61.
9. Ibid., 15.
10. Ibid., 13.
11. Ibid., 10–11.
12. Ibid.

13. Ibid., 12–13.
14. Ibid., 17.
15. Ibid., 19.
16. Ibid., 18.
17. Ibid.
18. Ibid., 23–24.
19. Ibid., 22–23.
20. Ibid., 23.
21. Ibid., 24–26.
22. Ibid., 27.
23. Ibid., 27–29.
24. Ibid., 29.
25. Ibid., 40–41.
26. Ibid., 31.
27. Ibid., 33.
28. Ibid., 34.
29. Ibid., 41–42.
30. Ibid., 48–49.
31. Ibid., 50.
32. Ibid., 51–52.
33. Ibid., 57–58.
34. Ibid., 58–59.

## Chapter 10. Dadisho Katraya

1. Brock, *Syriac Fathers*, 304.
2. A Guillaumont, "Dadisho Qatraya," *Dictionnaire de Spiritualité* 3 (Paris: Beauchesne, 1957): cols. 2–3.
3. Nedungatt, "Covenanters of the Holy Spirit," 207–8.
4. Dadisho Katraya, *A Treatise on Solitude*, in *Woodbrooke Studies* 7 (Cambridge: W. Heffer and Sons, Ltd., 1934): 70–76.
5. Ibid., 79.
6. Ibid., 82.
7. Ibid., 83.
8. Ibid., 84.
9. Ibid., 85–86.
10. Ibid., 97–98.
11. Ibid., 114–17.
12. Ibid., 117.
13. Ibid.
14. Ibid., 118–19.
15. Ibid., 120–22.
16. Ibid., 122.

## Chapter 11. Joseph and Abdisho Hazzaya

1. Beulay, "Joseph Hazzaya," *Dictionnaire de Spiritualité* 8 (Paris: Beauchesne, 1974): cols 1341–42.
2. Ibid., cols. 1347–49.
3. Ibid., cols. 1347–48.

4. Ibid., col. 1344.
5. Ibid., cols. 1344–45.
6. Ibid., col. 1345.
7. Abdisho Hazzaya, *Mystical Treatises*, in *Woodbrooke Studies* 7, A. Mingana, trans. (Cambridge: W. Heffer and Sons, Ltd., 1934): 170–71.
8. Beulay, "Joseph Hazzaya," col. 1345.
9. Ibid., cols. 1345–46.
10. Hazzaya, *Mystical Treatises*, 156.
11. Beulay, "Joseph Hazzaya," cols. 1345–46.
12. Hazzaya, *Mystical Treatises*, 152–55, 164, 171.
13. Brock, *Syriac Fathers*, 316–17.
14. Hazzaya, *Mystical Treatises*, 147–49.
15. Ibid., 149–50.
16. Ibid., 165–67.
17. Beulay, "Joseph Hazzaya," col. 1346.
18. Ibid., cols. 1346–47.
19. Hazzaya, *Mystical Treatises*, 150–52, 156.
20. Ibid., 156–60.
21. Ibid.

## Chapter 12. John of Dalyatha (John Saba)

1. Brock, *Syriac Fathers*, 329.
2. Beulay, "Jean de Dalyatha," *Dictionnaire de Spiritualité* 8 (Paris: Beauchesne, 1974): col. 451.
3. Ibid., col. 450.
4. Ibid., cols. 450–52.
5. Colless, "The Mysticism of John Saba," *Orientalia Christiana Periodica* 39 (Rome: Pontificium Institutum Orientalium Studiorum): 90, 96.
6. Beulay, "John de Dalyatha," col. 451.
7. Colless, "Mysticism of John Saba," 87.
8. Ibid., 89–90.
9. Brock, "Prayer of the Heart," 135–36.
10. Ibid., 138–39.
11. Ibid., 139.
12. Colless, "Mysticism of John Saba," 97.

## Appendix: Stephen Bar Sudaili

1. Hausherr, "De Doctrina Spirituali Christianorum Orientalium, questiones et scripta, I, no. 4, L'influence du 'Livre de Saint Hiérothée,'" *Orientalia Christiana* 30 (Rome: Pontificium Institutum Orientalium Studiorum, 1933): 28–35.
2. A. Guillaumont, "Étienne Bar Soudaili," *Dictionnaire de Spiritualité* 4 (Paris: Beauchesne, 1960): cols. 1486–88.
3. Hausherr, "De Doctrina Spirituali," 51–58.
4. A. Guillaumont, "Étienne Bar Soudaili," col. 1484.
5. Ibid.
6. Ibid.
7. Ibid., col. 1483.

8. Ibid., cols. 1484–85.

9. Ibid., col. 1485.

10. Windengren, "Researches in Syrian Mysticism, Mystical Experience and Spiritual Exercises," *Numen* 8 (London: Bril, 1961): 191–92.

11. Ibid., 194–95.

12. A. Guillaumont, 'Étienne Bar Soudaili,' cols. 1485–86.

13. Windengren, "Researches in Syrian Mysticism," 195.

14. Hausherr, "De Doctrina Spirituali," 39–40.

15. A. Guillaumont, "Étienne Bar Soudaili," col. 1486.

16. Ibid.

# Bibliography

Baker, Aelred. "Early Syrian Asceticism." *Downside Review* 88 (1970): 393–409.

———. "The 'Gospel of Thomas' and the Syriac 'Liber Graduum.' " *New Testament Studies* 12 (1965–66): 49–55.

———. "Syriac and the Origins of Monasticism." *Downside Review* 86 (1968): 342–53.

Bardy, Gustave. "Acedia." *Dictionnaire de Spiritualité* 1 (1937): cols. 166–69.

———. "Apatheia." *Dictionnaire de Spiritualité* 1 (1937): cols. 727–46.

Beck, Edmund. "Asceticisme et Monachisme chez St. Éphrem." *L'Orient Syrien* 3 (1958): 273–98.

Beggiani, Seely. *Early Syriac Theology.* Lanham, Md.: University Press of America, 1983.

Beulay, Robert. "Jean de Dalyatha." *Dictionnaire de Spiritualité* 8 (1974): col. 451.

———. "Joseph Hazzaya." *Dictionnaire de Spiritualité* 8 (1974): cols. 1341–49.

———. *La lumière sans forme. Introduction a la mystique chrétienne syro–orientale.* Chevetogne, 1987.

Blasucci, Antonio. "Images & Contemplation." *Dictionnaire de Spiritualitié* 7 (1971): cols. 1471–90.

Bradley, Bruce. "Jean le Solitaire." *Dictionnaire de Spiritualité* 8 (1974): cols. 764–72.

Brock, Sebastian. "Divine Call and Human Response: The Syriac Tradition II: St. Isaac of Nineveh." *The Way* (1981): 68–74.

———. "An Early Maronite Text on Prayer. *Parole de l'Orient* 13 (1986): 79–94.

———. "Early Syrian Asceticism." *Numen* 20 (1973): 1–19. Reprinted in *Syrian Perspectives on Late Antiquity.* London, 1984.

———. "Ephrem's Letter to Publius." *Le Muséon* 89 (1976): 216–305.

———. "Isaac de Ninive." *Lettre de Ligugé* 189: 16–25.

———. "John the Solitary on Prayer." *Journal of Theological Studies* 30 (1979): 84–101.

———. *The Luminous Eye: The Spiritual World Vision of St. Ephrem.* Rome: Centre for Indian and Inter–Religious Studies, 1985.

———. "The Prayer of the Heart in Syrian Tradition." *Sobornost* 4:2 (1982): 131–42.

———. "St. Isaac of Nineveh and Syriac Spirituality." *Sobornost* 7:2 (1975): 79–89.

———. *The Syriac Fathers on Prayer and the Spiritual Life.* Kalamazoo, Mich.: Cistercian Publications, 1987.

———. *Studies in Syriac Spirituality.* The Syrian Churches Series 13. Edited by Jacob Vellian. Poona, India: Anita Printers, 1988.

————. "The Syriac Tradition." In *The Study of Spirituality*. Edited by Cheslyn Jones, Geoffrey Wainwright and Edward Yarnold, S.J. Oxford and New York: Oxford University Press, 1986.

Burkitt, Francis Crawford. *Early Eastern Christianity*. London: 1904.

Camelot, Pierre–Thomas. "Lumière: Étude Patristique." *Dictionnaire de Spiritualité* 9 (1976): cols. 1149–58.

Campbell, Thomas L., trans. *Pseudo–Dionysius Areopagite: The Ecclesiastical Hierarchy*. Washington, D.C.: Catholic University of America Press, 1955.

Colless, Brian. "The Mysticism of John Saba." *Orientalia Christiana Periodica* 39 (1973): 83–102.

————. "The Place of Syrian Christian Mysticism in Religious History." *Journal of Religious History* 5 (1968): 1–15.

Drijvers, Hans J. W. "Hellenistic and Oriental Origins." In *The Byzantine Saint*. Edited by G. Sergei Hackel. *Studies Supplementary to Sobornost 5*. London: Fellowship of St. Alban and St. Sergius, 1981.

Gilson, Etienne. *History of Christian Philosophy in the Middle Ages*. New York: Random House, 1955.

Graffin, Francois. "Jacques de Saroug." *Dictionnaire de Spiritualité* 8 (1974): cols. 56–60.

Gribomont, Jean. "Le monachisme au sein de l'Église en Syrie et en Cappodoce." *Studia Monastica* 7 (1965): 7–24.

————. "Monasticism and Asceticism: Eastern Christianity." In *Christian Spirituality: Origins to the Twelfth Century*. Edited by Bernard McGinn, John Meyendorff and Jean Leclercq. New York: Crossroad, 1987.

Guillaumont, Antoine. *Aux origines du monachisme chrétien*. Spiritualité Orientale 30. Begrolles–en–Mauges: Abbaye de Bellfontaine, 1979.

————. "Dadisho Qatraya." *Dictionnaire de Spiritualité* 3 (1957): cols. 2–3.

————. "Étienne Bar Soudaili." *Dictionnaire de Spiritualité* 4 (1960): cols. 1481–86.

————. "Les 'arrhes de l'Esprit' dans le Livre des Degrées." In *Memorial Mgr. Gabriel Khouri–Sarkis*. Louvain: Imprimerie Orientaliste, 1969.

————. "Liber Graduum." *Dictionnaire de Spiritualité* 9. (1976): cols. 749–52.

————. "Situation et Signification du 'Liber Graduum' dans la spiritùalité Syriaque." *Orientalia Christiana Analecta* 197 (1974): 311–25.

Guillaumont, Antoine and Claire. "Évagre le Pontique." *Dictionnaire de Spiritualité* 4 (1960): cols. 1731–44.

————, eds. *Evagrius Ponticus*. Paris: Editions du Cerf, 1971.

Harb, Paul. "Doctrine spirituelle de Jean le Solitaire (Jean d'Apamée)." *Parole de l'Orient* 2 (1971): 225–60.

————. "L'Attitude de Philoxèn de Mabboug à l'égard de la Spiritualité 'Savante' d'Evagre le Pontique." In *Memorial Mgr. Gabriel Khouri–Sarkis*. Louvain: Imprimerie Orientaliste, 1969.

————. "Les origines de la doctrine de 'la-hasusuta' (Apatheia) chez Philoxène de Mabboug." *Parole de l'Orient* 5 (1974): 227–42.

Hausherr, Irenée. "Aphraat." *Dictionnaire de Spiritualité* 1 (1937): 746–52.

————. "Contemplation et Sainteté, une remarqueable mise au point par Philoxène de Mabboug (+523)." *Revue d'Ascètique et de Mystique* 14 (1933): 171–95.

————. "De Doctrina Spirituali et Scripta, I, No. 4: L'influence du 'Livre du Saint Hierothée.' " *Orientalia Christiana* 30 (1933): 176–211.

————. "Un grand auteur spirituel retrouvé: Jean d'Apamée." *Orientalia Christiana Analecta* 183 (1969): 187–216.

————. "Les grands courants de la spiritualité orientale." *Orientalia Christiana Periodica* 1 (1935): 114–38.

————. "Spiritualité Syrienne: Philoxène de Mabboug en version française." *Orientalia Christiana Periodica* 23 (1957): 171–85.

Hazzaya, Abdisho, *Mystical Treatises*. In *Woodbrooke Studies 7*, A. Mingana, trans. (Cambridge: W. Heffer and Sons, Ltd., 1934): 170–71.

Holy Transfiguration Monastery, trans. *The Ascetical Homilies of Saint Isaac the Syrian*. Boston: Holy Transfiguration Monastery, 1984.

Jargy, Simon. "Les 'fils et filles du pacte' dans la littérature monastique Syriaque." *Orientalia Christiana Periodica* 17 (1951): 304–20.

————. "Les Origines du Monachisme en Syrie et en Mesopotamie." *Proche–Orient Chrétien* 2 (1952): 110–24.

————. "Les Primiers Instituts Monastiques et les Principaux Representants du Monachisme Syrien au IVe Siècle." *Proche–Orient Chrétien* 4 (1954): 106–17.

Khalifé–Hachem, Elie. "Isaac de Ninive." *Dictionnaire de Spiritualité* 7 (1971): cols. 2041–54.

————. "La Prière pure et la prière spirituelle selon Isaac de Ninive." In *Memorial Mgr. Gabriel Khouri–Sarkis*. Louvain: Imprimerie Orientaliste, 1969.

Kirchmeyer, Jean. "Extase Chez les Pères de l'Église." *Dictionnaire de Spiritualité* 4:2 (1961): cols. 2087–2113.

Leloir, Louis. "Le pensée monastique d'Éphrem et Martyrius." *Orientalia Christiana Analecta* 197 (1973): 105–34.

————. "Martyrius (Sahdona)." *Dictionnaire de Spiritualité* 10 (1980): cols. 737–42.

Lemaitre, J., René Roques and M. Viller. "Contemplation Chez les Orientaux Chrétiens." *Dictionnaire de Spiritualité* 2 (1953): cols. 1762–1911.

Lemoine, Eugene. "La Spiritualité de Philoxène de Mabboug." *L'Orient Syrien* 2 (1957): 351–66.

Lossky, Vladimir. *The Mystical Theology of the Eastern Church*. Crestwood, N.Y.: St. Vladimir's Seminary Press, 1976.

Mingana, A., ed. and transl. *Early Christian Mystics*. In *Woodbrooke Studies 7*. Cambridge: W. Heffer and Sons, Ltd., 1934.

Murray, Robert. "Characteristics of the Earliest Syriac Christianity." In *East of Byzantium: Syria and Armenia in the Formative Period*. Edited by Nina G. Garsoian, Thomas F. Matthews and Robert Thomson. Washington, D.C.: Dumbarton Oaks, Center for Byzantine Studies, Trustees for Harvard University, 1982.

————. "The Exhortation to Candidates for Ascetical Vows at Baptism in the Ancient Syriac Church." *New Testament Studies* 21 (1974): 59–80.

————. "The Features of the Earliest Christian Asceticism." In *Christian Spirituality: Essays in Honor of E. Gordon Rupp*. Edited by Peter Brooks. London: S.C.M. Press, 1975.

————. "Recent Studies in Early Symbolic Theology." *Heythrop Journal* 6 (1965): 412–33.

————. "St. Ephrem the Syrian on Church Unity." *Eastern Churches Quarterly* 15 (1963): 164–73.

————. *Symbols of Church and Kingdom.* London: Cambridge University Press, 1975.

Nedungatt, George, S.J. "The Covenanters of the Early Syriac-Speaking Church." *Orientalia Christiana Periodica* 39 (1973): 191–215, 419–44.

Pseudo–Dionysius. *Pseudo–Dionysius: The Complete Works.* Translated by Colm Luibheid. Mahwah, NJ: Paulist Press, 1987.

Rayez, André. "Denys l'Aréopagite: Influence du Pseudo–Denys en Orient." *Dictionnaire de Spiritualité* 3 (1957): cols. 286–318.

Roques, René. "Dionysius l'Aréopagite." *Dictionnaire de Spiritualité* 3 (1957): cols. 243–86.

Simon of Taibutheh. *Mystical Works of Simon of Taibutheh.* In *Woodbrooke Studies* 7. Translated by A. Mingana. Cambridge: W. Heffer and Sons, Ltd., 1934.

Spearrit, Placid. *A Philosophical Enquiry into Dionysian Mysticism.* Dissertation, University of Fribourg, 1968.

Spidlik, Thomas. *La Spiritualité de l'Orient Chrétien, Orientalia Christiana Analecta.* Rome: Pontificium Institutum Orientalium Studiorum, 1978.

Voobus, Arthur. *History of Asceticism in the Syrian Orient II.* In *Corpus Scriptorum Christianorum Orientalium* 197, Subsidia Tome 17. Louvain, Secretariat du Corpus SCO, 1960.

————. "The Institution of the Benai Qeiama and Benat Qeiama in the Ancient Syrian Church." *Church history* 30 (1961): 19–27.

Watt, J. W. "Philoxenus and the Old Syriac Version of Evagrius' Centuries." *Oriens Christianus* 64 (1980): 65–81.

Wehbe, L. "Textes bibliques dan les écrits de Martyrios-Sahdona." *Melto* 5 (1969): 61–112.

Wensinck, J. *Mystic Treatises by Isaac of Nineveh.* Amsterdam, 1923.

Windengren, G. "Researches in Syrian Mysticism, Mystical Experience and Spiritual Exercise." *Numen* 8 (1961): 161–98.

# Index

Acedia, 44, 95, 109

Almsgiving, 29, 33

Amphiloqus of Iconium, 32

*Anagogic* movement, 56, 58, 59, 60, 61, 65

Angels, 23, 39, 52, 67, 103, 105; hierarchy of, 54, 55, 56, 57; of light, 85

*Apatheia* (impassibility), 44, 45, 49–51, 77–78, 82, 83, 84, 88, 97, 98

Aphraat, 13–28, 29, 48

Apophatism, 63, 65

Asceticism. *See* Corporeal stage of asceticism; Psychic stage of asceticism; Spiritual (pneumatic) stage of asceticism

Baker, Aelred, 29, 32

Baptism, 11, 16, 17, 18, 19, 21, 35, 37, 38, 52, 70, 74, 83, 95, 97, 101, 104; and chastity, 21, 23–24; and the contemplative life, 49, 50, 100; and divinization, 16; formative of the Church, 15–16, 20; and Messalianism, 33; and the moral life, 50; the new circumcision, 18; as sacrament of illumination, 60; of the Spirit, 31, 33, 34, 104; the "waters of testing," 17

Bar Hebraeus, 55, 99

Basil of Caesarea, 43, 67

Beck, Edmund, 20

Beulay, Robert, 94–95, 98

Black, Matthew, 18

*Bnai and Bnat Qyama*, 16–21, 22, 27, 29. *See* Sons and Daughters of the Covenant

Brock, Sebastian, 24, 41, 72, 101

Burkitt, Francis Crawford, 19

Cataphatic theology, 59

Celibacy, 17–20, 27, 30, 68

Charity. *See* Love

Circumcision of the heart, 17–20, 26

Church of the East, 7

Cloud of unknowing, 12, 62, 65

Commandments: obedience to the, 39, 44, 48, 50, 51, 82, 85, 87, 88, 95

Connolly, R. H., 19

Contemplation, 13, 43, 44, 45–46, 48, 49, 50, 51, 52, 58, 59, 60, 61, 62, 63–65, 66, 67, 70, 71, 78, 81, 82, 85, 88, 89, 91, 92, 93, 94, 96, 97, 98, 105, 110; of material beings, 45, 50, 73, 95–96; of rational or noncorporeal beings, 45, 50, 85, 95–96

Corporeal stage of asceticism, 11, 38–39, 42, 73–75, 94, 95–96, 100. *See* Somatic stage of asceticism

Creation: God's act of, 14–15, 36, 49, 56, 82, 83, 86, 87, 88, 89

Dadisho Katraya, 90–93

Darkness: mysticism of, 46, 54, 62, 63–65

Denis Bar Salibi, 55

Desert: living in the, 20, 21, 23, 24, 73, 91

Detachment, 39, 40, 44, 51, 63, 85. *See* Renunciation

Discernment, 77, 82, 85, 86

Discipleship: call to total, 11, 16, 18, 21, 28, 34

Divine Office, 21, 69, 91; canonical hours, 21; chanting the psalms, 42, 69, 73, 91, 92, 95, 96

Divinization (deification), 13, 14, 15, 16, 49, 54, 55, 56, 57, 59, 60, 63, 64, 65, 82, 101

Drijvers, Hans J. W., 20

Ecstasy, 46, 53, 54, 57, 60, 62–64, 79–80, 88, 97, 98. *See* Wonder

Encratists, 27

*Enkrateia*, 49–50